LET'S PLAY SOCCER

STAN LIVERSEDGE

octopus

First published 1979 by
Octopus Books Limited
59 Grosvenor Street
London W1

ISBN 0 7064 1004 1

Produced by
Mandarin Publishers Limited
22a Westlands Road,
Quarry Bay, Hong Kong

Printed in Singapore

CONTENTS

FOREWORD

Soccer is the most international game in the world; from the back streets of Sao Paulo to the public parks of Britain, from the beaches of Australia to the high schools of the United States – in fact, wherever there are a few children and a ball, makeshift goalposts are arranged and a game is soon in progress.

The skills and tactics needed in these impromptu matches are the same that are needed in top class games the world over. HOW TO PLAY SOCCER does what it sets out to do. It tells you in a clear, easy-to-understand way how to play your favourite game; how to control the ball, how to run with it, how to score goals, and how to prevent your opponents from scoring goals.

No matter how good you think you are, you can always improve, and this is the book to help you.

I hope that soccer will help to unite the people of the world as brothers in sport, peace and love.

In conclusion, in any sport, primarily in soccer, it is necessary to possess two great qualities; you must be a good athlete, but first you must be a person of good character.

INTRODUCTION

EDSON Arantes do Nascimento – Pele to you – called it 'the beautiful game'. Another famous personality once described it as 'a game of imagination and improvisation'. To the rest of the world it is the BIG-ball game . . . the game called Soccer.

It is a game watched by millions of people the world over, and played by youngsters from the moment they can kick a football around. Some youngsters – Pele, for instance, who in a career spanning 17 years scored more than 1,000 goals and became a legend in his own time – grow up to become world-famous and wealthy, because of their ability to do what comes naturally . . . kick a ball and almost 'make it talk'.

This book is designed to help YOU, by showing you how to improve your football, by giving you examples of the right way to do things, while at all times keeping it simple. Because, basically, Soccer IS a simple game, although as you progress, you find that training, practice and dedication can help you to improve upon the skills you already possess.

Every youngster who dreams of becoming a professional footballer must have ambition, as well as ability. Ambition to play not only for a top-class professional club, but for his country. Naturally, when you think of playing for your country, you think of playing in the greatest sports tournament in the world – the World Cup. And there are footballers who began by kicking a cloth ball around and wound up as World Cup stars.

The World Cup has been played in Argentina, Mexico, West Germany, Switzerland, Sweden, Chile, Brazil, Uruguay, France, Italy and England, and when England won the trophy in 1966 at Wembley, it was appropriate. Not just because England proved to be the best team; but because many people around the world regard England as the home of football.

The game in England had been thriving long before the Federation Internationale de Football Association – known simply as FIFA – came into being in 1904. It was a Frenchman, Jules Rimet (he became president of FIFA in 1921) who inspired the idea of the World Cup, and the first tournament took place in Uruguay in 1930. Now we eagerly anticipate the World Cup every four years.

In addition to FIFA, the world's governing body, there is the Union of European Football Associations – UEFA – which handles the big club competitions such as the European Cup, the UEFA Cup and the Cup-winners Cup, and in Britain there are bodies such as the Football Association, and the Football League each of which has different responsibilities while working together on many aspects of the game.

So you can see that, whether you are a spectator or a player, even at the lowest level in amateur football, you play a part in the overall scheme of

things so far as this great game is concerned. And if it is your ambition to become a successful professional footballer, you will, should you succeed, become ever more closely involved with Soccer.

The one thing which everyone in the game readily admits – and this includes players who have become known as stars – is that you can always find something new to learn from and about football. The game has rules of its own; it also has terms of its own; and while many people talk glibly in those terms, not everyone understands what he is talking about, even though he may think it sounds good.

We hope and believe that this book will enable you not only to talk and think about the game, but

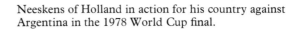

exactly what it says – the major league in the country. It is powerful, because it provides all the players who play for England . . . and internationals provide the greatest source of money for the Football Association.

'Over the years, there was some friction between the League and the FA, but this has settled down now because most members of the Football League's management committee – which is a far smaller body than the FA Council – are members of the Council, as well. There are 80 members of the Council, because every county has a representative, and all aspects of Football Association business are split up and dealt with by various committees. These cover finance, discipline, rules and regulations, internationals and so on. All decisions are made by the appropriate committees, and passed to the full Council for approval. Very rarely does the Council go against the recommendations of one of its committees.

'The FA international committee chooses the England team manager, and that committee has eight members, including myself. This committee is in charge of the England Under-21 side and the full England team. So you can see that quite a lot of work is involved through the year.

'The Football League is responsible for running the affairs of the 92 League clubs, and it looks after contracts, negotiations with the Professional Footballers' Association – the player's union – transfers, deals with the television people and the Pools companies, and generally bringing as much money as possible into League football.

'The League and the FA rely on each other in many respects, and they go together, although sometimes there can be a difference of opinion or, for someone like myself, a conflict of interest. As the chairman of Manchester City, I tend to think about my club first – that's the bread and butter, as it were – but, fortunately, usually what the clubs want is what is right for football.

'As a football administrator, I think it was only right that we should have looked closely at allowing foreign players into League football – although, as a club chairman with the aim of doing the best possible for my club and its supporters, I wanted to be able to get a work permit to bring a player from abroad, as when we negotiated for the transfer of Kasimierz Deyna, the Polish World Cup player. And both the Football League and the Football Association had passed a rule allowing two foreign players per club. Every change of rule has to be finalized by the Football Association but, as you can see, if the League clubs decide to admit a foreign player, the FA would go along with them. Generally speaking, both the League and the Football Association do a great deal together to keep the game going in good shape, at all levels.'

to understand the main points of it, to improve your knowledge and skill . . . while never forgetting that football, in essence, is still the same, simple game it was more than a century ago. As the Americans, who have so recently taken up the game, so aptly put it, Soccer remains 'a kick in the grass'.

Peter Swales is not only the chairman of one of England's top League clubs, Manchester City; he is a member of the Football Association Council, and he explains the difference between the FA and the Football League like this: 'The Football Association is the ruling body of Soccer responsible for all football in the country. The Football League is

TRAINING AND BALL CONTROL

Fitness

If you play football, you need to be as fit as possible. You need to build up strength, stamina and speed, and with this in mind, here are some suggestions which can help you . . . and you don't need expensive or complicated equipment.

For instance, you can do some fitness training on your way to or coming home from school. All you need is to be keen enough to get in some exercise. And remember, when it comes to stamina and the ability to last through 90 minutes (or even 80 minutes) of a football match, your feet and legs have to keep going.

So on your way to school, simply sprint from one lamp standard to the next, then jog to the third lamp standard, then sprint again to the fourth, and keep alternating between sprints and jogging until you reach school. And repeat the process on your way home. You may find at first that after a few sprints and jogging sections, you are out of breath and unable to complete the 'course' . . . in which case, when you really feel you've had enough, make a point of walking the distance between the next set of lamp standards. It's no good killing yourself to the point where you are exhausted.

If you make this a daily part of your routine, you should find that as time goes by – and very quickly, too – you can increase the distance you cover sprinting and jogging, and make the walking bits less frequent. If you live close by a park or even if you live in a built-up residential area, you can still add to your fitness by going out on a run after school two or three times a week, with the object of increasing that stamina still further. It should also help to speed you up, because the idea is that you time yourself.

Set out to see how much ground you can cover in 12 minutes; and gradually you will find that you are able to run further and further, still keeping inside the 12-minute schedule. If you can make your 12-minute run over ground which is as varied as possible, so much the better. You may find that you can cover half a mile comfortably at a steady jog, then do a sprint – up a rise or a hill if the ground is suitable for this. You can vary the run so that it does not get boring – sprint 15 or 20 yards (14–18 metres) and then jog the same distance. Remember again – in the early stage of this routine, do not be too proud to walk for a short spell to enable you to get that 'second wind'.

One thing: when you do those sprints, whether coming home from school or during a run round the park or the block, put everything you have into it. For in a football match, the ability to make ground quickly over the first few yards can often enable you to get to the ball before your opponent.

Here is some advice as to when to concentrate on the stamina work and when to put the accent on the sprinting. Try to complete your stamina programme before the Soccer season begins. You can

Below: The 'V' sit, lie flat on your back with your legs straight and your arms by your side. Raise your legs in the air, keeping them straight, and lift your head and back towards your legs into a V position. Hold this position for the count of five and then relax. Repeat five times at first gradually increasing this as you become fitter.

Below: The squat thrust, lie flat on your stomach and push your body up with your arms. Keeping your arms straight kick your legs forward into a crouch position (below right). Repeat five times and then increase this number as you gain strength.

There are many exercises that you can do with a chair. But make sure that the chair is quite secure and will not move as you work. Do the exercises shown here in rotation. Start off doing each one five times at first and repeat the circuit five times.

Below: When you are doing high-arm press-ups, make sure that you keep your feet apart and your body straight.

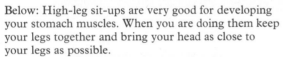

Below: High-leg sit-ups are very good for developing your stomach muscles. When you are doing them keep your legs together and bring your head as close to your legs as possible.

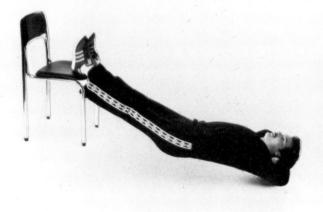

do this during the summer months when you're on holiday from school, so that by the time football starts, you have built up your stamina and can then concentrate on the 'spot' work, the idea being to add to the stamina by making sure you are fast off the mark. So during the season, it's a case of the more sprints the better.

If you are able to do some fitness training at a local Soccer ground or sports centre, you can develop your programme even more. For instance, you can jog to the half-way line, then sprint the other half of the pitch, then walk or jog round the back of the goal, jog down the other side of the field to the half-way line, and then finish up with as fast a sprint as possible.

You can also practise sprinting over various distances. Put down a coat or use the corner flag as the starting point, and put down four markers at intervals of five yards (four-and-a-half metres). Then sprint to the first marker, turn quickly and sprint back to the starting point; then sprint to the second marker, turn quickly and race back to the starting point; then it's a sprint to the third marker, and again a quick turn-round and back to the starting point; and finally go the whole hog – sprint flat out to the fourth marker, turn as quickly as you can, and leg it back to the starting point.

Although you may already have built up your stamina with that pre-season running over distances, it is a good thing to vary the training during

Below: Step-ups are very good for building up your
leg muscles and developing the staying power
necessary for lasting the full ninety minutes of a game.

The back press-up with a chair is tremendous for building
up the back muscles as well as the arms. They are quite
tiring and may take some getting into, so if you feel that you
are straining yourself too much, stop and relax before
carrying on.

the season and give yourself a reminder that you
have still got to last the distance in a game. So
maybe once a month you can introduce a long-
distance run into your schedule. And the chances
are that you will be doing some cross-country
running during the school terms, anyway.

Again, there's an old saying in football that you
must be careful not to leave all your strength on the
training ground – the idea is to build up to peak
fitness for the game itself. So if you are doing some
distance running – maybe round a Soccer pitch –
put in two slow laps and two quick laps, and keep a
record of your times over distances of between one
mile and two miles (1,500 and 3,000 metres). You
will find you can cover the distance quicker.

If you have a friend who is keen to go fitness
training with you, you can work together by doing
shuttle runs. For instance, you can make it five sets
of sprints down half the length of the pitch, and
three sets of sprints down the full length of the
pitch. You start from the corner flag and sprint to
the half-way line, then he goes from there to the
other end of the pitch; then you retrace your steps
the moment he has reached his end, and so on, so
that each of you is alternating. As you stop, he goes;
as he stops, you go. And, of course, you can vary
the routines to suit yourself . . . but always with
the accent on improving your fitness and the times
over the various distances.

Of course, it is not always possible to get out to a

track or a football field to get in some running. You may not have the time to spare, or the weather may be too bad. But that need not stop you from at least maintaining your fitness – and building up the various muscles. Indeed, you can work at it without even leaving the house. All you need is a chair or a stool, and you can do a variety of exercises.

No doubt you have done press-ups in your school gymnasium or during the physical-training period. So carry on with the press-ups while you are at home – but as well as doing the normal press-ups on the floor do them using a chair, as demonstrated in the pictures. You can have your feet on the floor, and your hands behind you on the chair, which means you're doing back press-ups; or you can have your feet on the chair and your body facing down to the floor, and do the press-ups that way. You can also practise step-ups, using a chair or a low stool or a bench, and this kind of exercise builds up the leg muscles, too. And you can do 'squat' exercises and thrusts, and exercises which build up body muscles and, at the same time, make your limbs even more supple.

Footballers need ability and skill, but they also have to be athletes, to a very large extent, and there is scarcely a muscle in the body which they do not need to use at some time or another during a game. The simple exercises we have illustrated will help you to improve your all-round fitness and build up the muscles in the legs, the stomach, the neck and the arms. Remember, you use your arms to help propel you when you run; you need power in the neck muscles when you are handling the ball; you need strength in the leg muscles for 'taking off' and for pounding across the turf.

You may have heard of the term *work rate* in football, and a lot of unkind things have been said about this – such as, 'Players can produce work rate, but they've lost out on the skill'. Obviously, it is no good being a carthorse when the need is for a thoroughbred, but the fact remains that a game of football is not a five-minute affair. It is a demanding hour and a half under all kinds of conditions.

Certainly he has to work at improving his skill as a footballer. One FA coach puts the emphasis on this quite clearly, because he says: 'Mastering the ball is the No. 1 factor, in my view, and I stress this to all the boys I coach. I want them first and foremost to be able to control the ball, to pass and shoot accurately, and develop the skill which is vital. But having said that, never forget that skill must be accompanied by physical fitness, so that you have the strength to last through a game and apply the skills you possess for the benefit of your team. It's no good being able to control the ball if your opponent is beating you to it every time, and it's no good being able to play for 75 minutes if you have to give up, physically, for the last 15 minutes. You've got to be able to keep on repeating the physical effort in a game, cover a vast amount of the pitch – and that demands real fitness.'

Training

Training with the ball is the most important thing of all. Physical fitness can be catered for largely within school time, when you do physical education lessons and, as we mentioned earlier you can build up your physical fitness during your own time by the use of simple exercises and routines. If you are a good player, you will get plenty of chance to maintain physical fitness by training with the school team, or playing in matches. But training with the ball, and learning to master it under virtually any conditions, is what counts first. And you can improve your skills and control of the ball even when you are on your own.

You can practise kicking a ball against a wall, standing five to ten yards (four-and-half to nine metres) away, and hitting the rebound first time. See how many times you can do that without having to stop the ball in order to control it, and without letting it rebound past you. When you

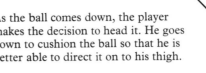

As the ball comes down, the player makes the decision to head it. He goes down to cushion the ball so that he is better able to direct it on to his thigh.

have done a spell of kicking the ball against the wall, keeping the ball on the ground, try to kick it through the air against the wall, and see how often you can kick the ball back, first time, without it touching the ground. What you're doing in the first instance is practising passing along the ground and receiving the ball from a team-mate (the wall). In the second instance you are volleying the ball.

You can stand five to ten yards (four-and-a half to nine metres) from the wall and hit the ball into the wall fairly high, then you have to control the ball when it rebounds. Repeat time and again, kicking the ball harder and harder, and all the time, as soon as the ball rebounds, control it as quickly as possible, setting yourself up for the next drive.

You can try this, standing ten yards (nine metres) from the wall, and gradually increasing the distance between you and the wall, all the time hitting the ball harder and harder. It takes time to perfect this, so do not be disheartened if, at first, any of the training tips appear difficult. With

practice you find that every move comes more easily, and eventually you can do some of the things without even having to think about it.

Practice makes perfect, but variety is the spice of life, and it is the spice of training routines, too. So when you have practised kicking the ball against the wall for a while, throw it against the wall instead, and try controlling the rebound with your thigh, your chest or your head, bringing the ball down to the ground again and kicking it back against the wall, trying to vary the height so that you are controlling the ball with different parts of the body before bringing it down to the foot, kicking it against the wall again, and repeating the 'circular'.

But, of course, it is not sufficient to control the ball when you are merely standing still. Once you have become proficient in this aspect, you have to remember that during a game players of your own team – and the opposition – are constantly on the move . . . so you will need to be on the move

17

yourself. Otherwise, an opponent will surely take the ball from you. So you start all over again, this time working your way along the wall and still trying to control the ball as it rebounds, keeping on the move as you would during a game.

It is important, also, that you are not a one-footed player. Every footballer has a favourite foot, but the idea is that you should be able to use both feet during a match, and so when you are passing the ball against the wall – standing for a start maybe five yards (four-and-a-half metres) from it – get used to the idea of hitting the ball with the right foot and then the left foot, in turn, still keeping it under control. Practise this standing still, at first, then start moving down the wall as you become more expert at controlling the ball.

Now you will come back to throwing the ball against the wall, this time with the idea of improving your heading ability. Throw the ball so that when it rebounds, you must jump into the air to reach it with your head – and, of course, the idea is that you head it back against the wall, and try to keep on doing this without letting the ball touch the ground.

Here is another example of controlling the ball: take it on your instep, flick it a few inches in the air, and see if you can collect it again on the instep on your other foot . . . then flick it in the air again, and let it drop to the instep of the first foot. Keep on doing this, and see how many times you can transfer the ball from one instep to another without letting it touch the ground. You may do it only three or four times for a start, but with practice you can do it up to 100 times or even more, without the ball once touching the ground.

So, when you have accomplished that little trick, you think you know it all? – Try flicking the ball from the instep to the thigh, then letting it drop back to the instep without touching the ground. Then go on to something even more ambitious . . . from instep to thigh to chest to head, and back to chest, to thigh, to instep. And keep on repeating this move as many times as possible, without letting the ball touch the ground.

Watch any team when they go out for the kickabout before a game. There will be at least one player who does this trick or some variation of it . . . and you may even see a player flick the ball from his instep to the thigh, then to his chest, then to his head . . . and let the ball roll over the back of his head until it is resting in the 'crook' of his neck as he leans forward. Then he will flick the ball back on to the top of his head, down to his chest, to his thigh and back to his instep.

There is also a move which people in the game call the midfield man's turn, and Liverpool's star striker, Kenny Dalglish, is an expert at this. Kevin Keegan used to do a variation of it, as well.

Stand about ten yards (nine metres) from the wall, and play the ball against the wall, on the ground. Collect the rebound, control it and turn in

Not being in a position to head the ball, the player decides to take it on his chest. He braces himself for contact and draws his chest in to reduce the impact. Having stopped the ball on his chest and then drops it onto his foot, to make a pass or start a run.

one movement. If you collect the ball with the left foot, you turn with it to your left; if you collect it with your right foot, you turn to your right. You take the ball on your instep as it comes back to you off the wall, and it is the quickest way to turn with the ball and leave an opponent standing as he is trying to mark you. Or you can take the ball with the outside of the foot, feint with your body as if you are going one way, then flick the ball the other way and turn quickly in that direction. Keegan really is an expert at making this little trick pay off.

You do not need a wall – or even a team-mate – to practise dribbling – and remember, controlling the ball while you are moving is an important part of

the game. You can put down coats or bricks at short distances, then run with the ball at your feet, twisting and turning between the markers as if you were dribbling past an opponent. Or you can dribble up to the marker and turn quickly, then go to the next marker and turn the opposite way.

When you reach the end marker, turn round straight away, still controlling the ball, and repeat the exercise. Or you can take the ball up to the first marker, turn quickly and go back to your starting point, then dribble up to the next marker, repeat the drill, and continue this until you have reached the last marker, still turning quickly from there and going back to your starting point. A variation of

an opponent push the ball between his legs and leave him standing by nipping round him to gain possession and race away with the ball – so it is a trick which, while it looks great when it does come off, cannot be repeated too often during a game. Once bitten, the defender will be twice shy!

Heading the ball is an important part of the game, especially for a defender, and the ball can come at you from any direction during a match. You can improve your heading by practising, and your judgment by anticipating the rebound. So throw the ball against the wall, then stand still and head it back. That is relatively easy. Then throw the ball higher against the wall so that you have to jump when you head it back. That's not too difficult, either.

But now try another heading routine. Throw the ball against the wall and head the rebound into the air. Keep heading the ball in the air as you're standing still, but each time you nod the ball upwards, go down so that eventually you are squatting on your haunches, still heading the ball in the air. Keep the ball in the air with your head as you slowly regain a standing position – and if you don't let the ball touch the ground once, then well done! Oh, yes . . . once you've regained that standing position, head the ball against the wall, then take the rebound and repeat the whole drill. See how many times you can do this routine without letting the ball hit the ground.

You can also test the accuracy of your heading – and your passing – by putting chalk marks on the wall and aiming your header or pass at the chalk mark, while standing about ten yards (nine metres) from the wall. Once you find that you are hitting the target regularly, make it that little bit harder for yourself by moving further and further away from the wall, still trying to hit the target. And, just for fun, award yourself marks out of ten for direct hits on the chalk mark.

You will find that when you are kicking the ball towards the chalk mark on the wall, the further you move from the wall the longer the distance and, therefore, the harder the pass, which tends to become higher and higher so that, in the end, you are hitting a lofted drive.

In this chapter, we have illustrated how you can improve your control of the ball without really needing assistance from team-mates, and the aim all the time is to put the lessons you have learned into action during a game. You have been given some tips on controlling the ball and turning quickly, to either side, on gaining accuracy in passing and heading, and on getting up quickly from a static position. So now we'll deal with situations where two or more of you can work out moves during practice sessions.

this routine is to dribble up to the marker, put your foot on the ball to trap it, then turn quickly and dribble back with the ball.

If you are practising dribbling and have a team-mate to bar your way, see if you can 'nutmeg' him – and how often you can do it, once he knows what you are up to. The idea is that you slip the ball between his legs as he prepares to challenge you, then you go round him and get possession of the ball again. One famous player was so pleased at nutmegging his brother who was playing on the opposite side, that he kept on shouting at him 'I nutmegged you . . . I nutmegged you.'

Naturally, no defender is pleased when he sees

Together

Two heads may – or may not – be better than one, but certainly when you're practising training routines it's handy if you have a team-mate to get involved with you. Or even a few more friends, so that you can get up a five-a-side game. But even if there are just two of you on the playing field or in the park, you can help each other to perfect ball control and passing, heading and shooting.

We have discussed passing against a wall, but you can use your partner as the 'wall', especially when it comes to passing and controlling the ball. Stand ten yards (nine metres) from each other, and when you pass the ball, make sure that it is accurate and goes to your partner's feet; then he can knock the ball back first time to you, and you return the compliment, touching the ball only once as you make the passes.

From there, you can progress to passing the ball so that it reaches your partner and he has to control it with his thigh, his chest or his head, before he kicks the ball back to you – and then you have to control it with the thigh, chest or head. You can have a competition, seeing who controls the ball most accurately and how many times you can make the passes without losing the ball.

You can vary the practice, by throwing the ball to your partner, who stands about five yards (four-and-a-half metres) away, so that he has to head it back to you and, if possible, you head the ball back to him. Again, you keep a score on who is able to continue this heading game the longest. Or you can dribble the ball against each other, trying to 'nutmeg' one another, depending on which of you has possession, and you can also practise taking a throw-in, with your partner moving further and further away each time you take the throw. Each throw you take, of course, has to be headed or quickly controlled by your partner, and the same applies when you are the receiver.

Then the pair of you can stand 20 yards (18 metres) apart, and when you pass to him you run forward to take the return pass, then repeat the performance, passing back to him, until you have both covered half the length of the pitch. You can also throw the ball to your partner (standing five yards apart) and he has to head it in the air, then nod it back to you, and you do exactly the same, before heading the ball back to him. This means that all the time, you are gaining experience in controlling the ball in the air.

Another move you can practise: stand three or four yards (two or three metres) in front of your partner, throw the ball so that it reaches him knee-high, but to his right or left, which means he has to volley the ball back to you with his instep. Then he does the same for you, which means both of you are gaining experience in controlling the ball with either side, and improving your footwork.

Here's another move you can practise together.

As the low ball approaches, the player drops his thigh to take the ball. When the ball hits the thigh, the leg is drawn back so that the ball is brought down to the ground in a well-controlled way.

Face each other, five yards (four-and-a-half metres) apart – but as you run forward, he runs backward, while you play the ball to his feet and he gives you a return, first-time pass. And another variation: get your partner to throw the ball to you from 10 or 15 yards (9–14 metres) and you have to keep it in the air with any part of your body except your hands until you have reached him. Then see if he can do the same.

All the time, as you become more proficient in the various training routines, keep on thinking about making it more difficult for yourself, so that you're always striving to improve upon your past performances. For instance, once you have mastered the art of kicking the ball when it is stationary, get your partner to throw it to you so that you have to control the ball when it comes at you from different directions. And if there are three of you, get one partner to go in goal while the other two of you enjoy a bit of shooting practice.

In this case, you and your partner can run

alongside each other, passing the ball to and fro, until you reach a certain spot inside the 18-yard box – and when that happens, the player with the ball shoots for goal. Or you can have your partner throwing the ball to you so that you have to hit it on the volley for goal, just as often happens in a match, when the ball drops into the box and a striker has just a split second in which to volley a shot for the target – otherwise he'll have a defender breathing down his neck.

Do not forget that during a game, you are often under pressure, and if three of you are practising moves, you can get the 'keeper to throw the ball out to your partner while you go up with him to challenge for the header. Then the 'keeper can throw the ball to you, and your partner has to see if he can win the airborne duel. If there are just two of you, get your partner to go in goal, while you stand on the edge of the box; then throw the ball in the air and – before it has travelled five yards (four-and-a-half metres) ahead of you – hit it for goal. It must

not have bounced more than once before you hit it.

There is yet another move which is aimed at improving your accuracy and your speed off the mark. Stand facing your partner and, as he throws the ball over your head and behind you, turn quickly, run forward and hit the ball into goal before it has bounced twice. It helps, too, of course, if there is someone to act as 'aunt sally' by playing the goalkeeper's role.

The 'keeper can get into the practice session also by throwing the ball out accurately, as he would do to a defender during a game, and to give the goalkeeper more practice you can throw the ball to your partner inside the six-yard box, so that he goes up to head for goal – with the 'keeper coming out to try to catch the ball or punch clear before your partner can score. You can also practise shooting from the penalty spot, and you then have to decide if you can trick the goalkeeper either by placing your shot beyond his reach – try to kid him by making him dive one way, while you hit the ball to the opposite side of goal – or by hammering the ball so hard that he simply cannot stop it. But remember that in either case, it's vital to shoot as accurately as possible.

If you can get hold of three footballs, line them up on the edge of the penalty area and put a marker about five yards (four-and-a-half metres) outside the area, so that the marker and the footballs form a triangle. Then you race from the marker, hit one ball for goal, race back to the marker, run and hit the next ball for goal, go back to the marker and return to hit the third ball for goal. This helps you to get into the swing of taking quick action when you are under pressure during a game.

If three of you are practising, you can try the 'con trick'. In this instance, the goalkeeper and defender stand on the goal line and the attacker stands on the edge of the six-yard box, facing away from goal, with three footballs lined up on the edge of the 18-yard box.

As soon as the attacker moves towards one of the footballs, the defender can advance from the goal line towards him. The attacker reaches a ball, turns with it and dribbles towards goal, trying to get past the defender and shoot, or shooting first time before the defender can reach him. If the defender manages to play the ball out of the penalty area, he has won it; if the goalkeeper saves the attacker's shot, the ball is 'dead', but if the 'keeper only parries the ball, the attacker can go for the rebound and have another shot. Each time, the attacker takes his pick of the three footballs which have been set down on the edge of the 18-yard box. So if you are the attacker, see how many goals you can score out of three. And, of course, you switch places after that, so that you become the defender or the 'keeper, so you get all-round practice.

From a goalkeeper's point of view, the shot which is struck low and hard towards the corner of the net is the most difficult one for him to save – so practise shooting hard, low . . . and accurately, especially on the run. Do not neglect to practise volleying the ball, either – often, in a game, you do not get time to bring the ball down and go for the low shot; you just have to hit it first time when the ball is on the volley.

When you have a few team-mates to take part in a small-sided game, three of you can practise this move: one player stands in the middle, with a player ten yards (nine metres) either side of him. The man in the middle has the ball, and he runs with it towards one of the other players. When he gets five yards (four-and-a-half metres) away, he pushes the ball towards that player, who knocks the ball ten yards (nine metres) behind the man who has made the pass, so that he has to turn quickly, run and collect the ball, and pass it to the third player. Practise this move ten times, then let one of the other players become the man in the middle.

Small-sided games, which means anything from three a side to seven a side, are ideal for perfecting footballing skills. It takes eleven men to make a team, but many of the top players in the game today learned the basic trade of football – and helped to perfect their skills – by playing in small-sided games and pitting their wits, their physical fitness and their natural ability against lads of their own age group. Even if only half a dozen of you turn up, you can get together and work on moves such as we have described here, and all the time you will become better players for doing so.

Flair

If you have a natural flair for doing something well, then you start off with a big advantage. When it comes to playing Soccer, every hopeful has SOME strong point, as well as weak points. An experienced manager told me once upon a time: 'Nothing gives me greater pleasure than seeing a youngster who cost nothing break through to regular first-team football . . . especially if he's managed to make the most of his natural flair.'

That manager had a theory which he always tried to put into practice, whenever his club signed a boy straight from school. The boy had already been watched often by the club, and he might well have played for his school team, his county side and even his country, as a schoolboy. When he arrived at the club, the manager would watch him being put through his paces during the early days, and look particularly for any natural strong points in the lad's play.

'If he could kick strongly and accurately with his left foot, I made sure my training and coaching staff not only knew it, too, but that they made certain that, so far as possible, the lad never made a mistake when he kicked with his left. In other words, they did their best to help the boy perfect doing what came naturally to him . . . then they tried to strengthen his weak spots. And all the time, they kept it simple, making sure he knew what was going on.'

Usually, if a boy is good at one sport, he is useful at several games, although he will be stronger in one branch of sport than others. In the same way, a Soccer hopeful will have one or two strong points which are a natural gift. Maybe trapping a ball comes easily to him, or he has that initial speed off the mark which enables him to win the race to the ball. Perhaps he has a natural body swerve which will take him past an opponent – or if he is a goalkeeper the ability to kick the ball almost into his opponents' goalmouth. As the manager said, when the strong points are already there, and come naturally to the young player, make sure they

Right: Mike Channon playing for England against Scotland is one of the best examples of a player with natural flair. He is seen here taking the ball round the defender, setting himself up for a deep, offensive pass.

remain. And practise, practise, practise . . . until practice makes perfect.

There are things in football which come only with experience. Such as reading a game. But even here, one youngster may well have greater vision than another. So he has a head start in this direction, and his reading of a game will improve still further, with experience.

What is reading of a game? It is the ability to see things developing during the course of play, to realize before others what is about to happen – or what can be made to happen. It is the ability to size up situations, even if you are not involved in the move that is going on at that particular moment, and become aware of where the next piece of action is liable to take place.

That's how a goal poacher gets round the 'blind side' of the defence and tucks away a scoring chance before other players have realized it's there. That's how a defender appears 'from nowhere' to clear a dangerous situation or maybe make a goal-line interception as the ball looks certain to go into the net.

There are 22 players on a football pitch, and you know that only two of them – the respective goalkeepers – will remain in more or less fixed positions. The other 20 players are constantly moving around, just as the ball moves around – and sometimes a player may be caught out because, instead of keeping his eyes open and his brain ticking away, he is guilty of what the professionals call 'ball-watching'. He's been so busy watching the ball that he has not noticed the man sneaking into position for where the ball is going to go. And when he does realize what's happened, it is too late.

Whatever the course of the action, not one of the 20 outfield players can be covering every blade of grass at the same time. Always there are bound to be spaces around the field; and if you have what is known as a footballing brain, you will soon realize that there is use to be made of the vacant spaces on a football field, just as there is use to be made of the ball when it is in your possession.

Imagine that you are a winger out on the flank, and the full-back has been keeping such a close watch on you that it's hard work getting past him. Every time you get a pass the full-back is standing virtually on your toes, or even breathing down your neck as the ball arrives. But if you spot one of your midfield team-mates has the ball, and you drift away from the full-back into one of the spaces on the field, you have a real chance of getting away from your marker . . . providing your midfield team-mate is tuned to the same mental wavelength and puts the ball into the right space at the right time . . . the time that you're arriving there.

That is an instance of what is known as reading the game, having vision, being able to see one move ahead, like an expert chess player. It gives you a head start on your opponent, if you learn to read the game correctly and quickly.

To control the ball with the instep of the foot as it approaches, drop your leg as the ball comes to your foot. Relax the foot a little so that as the ball comes to your instep you are ready to keep the ball under firm control.

The leg movements to control the ball with the outside of the foot are virtually the same as they are for controlling with the instep. The player in this sequence takes a fairly high ball and controls it beautifully, turning smoothly in virtually the same movement.

TACTICS AND PASSES

Formations

In the old days of Soccer, it used to be simple: a team had a goalkeeper, two full-backs, three half-backs and five forwards, and we called it the W-M formation. The full-backs had the job of stopping attacks down the wings, the centre-half-back was the man who bottled up attacks coming through the middle, and the half-backs defended and prompted attacking moves by their own forwards.

Over the past ten years or so, we have seen team formations change, and we hear a lot of talk about 4-3-3, 4-2-4 and 4-4-2. I have even seen sides which had their own, somewhat surprising team formations featuring five men strung out in a line ahead of the goalkeeper and three players in front of them, leaving just two men upfield, and often I have seen sides playing with a 'sweeper' between the goalkeeper and the defence, or between the defence and the attack.

So what does it all mean? – Let's get this team-formation business in perspective; in other words, let us put the thing in simple terms. And we'll start by saying that, whatever the formation, ignore the goalkeeper, because he's the one man who is static, who stays exactly where he is, and does not figure in the formation.

It does not matter whether it's 4-3-3, 4-2-4 or 4-2, the first figure '4' refers to the defenders. They are known as the back-four men, and they are simply two full-backs, one playing wide on the right, the other on the left, and between them two central defenders, instead of the one-time single centre-half.

So 4-3-3 means four men – the two full-backs and the two central defenders – playing in a line across the field in front of the 'keeper; three players occupying midfield positions in a line across the pitch in front of them; and three attackers in a line across the field up front.

If it's 4-2-4, you have the back-four line again, two men playing in midfield, and four attackers; and if it's 4-4-2, you have the back-four line, four men in midfield, and just two attackers.

The thirds of the football field. The centre third is area of preparation and build up, and the other two are the areas of attacking and defending.

4-3-3

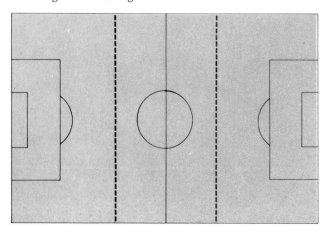

There is no doubt about one thing: Soccer is very much a team game, and this means that every member of the side playing in an outfield position has to be prepared to switch and move around as the game goes on, because football is never at a standstill, and often players may move out of their defensive or midfield areas to join in attacks, while forwards may have to drop back to help their own defence when it is under pressure from the opposition. The one exception, as I said, is the goalkeeper.

In one way, he occupies the least-glamorous position in the side (how often have YOU volunteered to keep goal?) . . . yet in another, he can turn out to be the star attraction. For when everyone else has failed, he alone stands between the opposition and a goal. If he lets in a 'soft one' or makes a mistake which leads to a goal, everyone blames him; if he brings off a marvellous save, everyone applauds and says he's won the match for his team.

There may be lengthy spells when play is at the other end of the field (and it may be a bitterly cold day or a warm afternoon). but the goalkeeper always has to be on the alert for an attack suddenly developing. Of course, he hopes his back-four men will stop play getting that far . . . and, indeed, they are there to bar the route to goal.

The back-four men usually are strong tacklers, capable of winning the ball from an attacking opponent; they are often fast themselves, capable of recovering quickly and having another go, if beaten once. The two central defenders, especially, are expected to be good at winning the ball in the air, and between them, all four men playing at the back develop an understanding as they play more and more together, so that each man learns how the other plays his game, and can fit in accordingly.

Soccer is simple, so instead of giving the ball the 'big boot' when they win it, the back-four men usually try the short pass to their midfield men, whose job then is to set their own forwards on the attack. Usually one midfield man, at least, is known as a 'ball-winner', which means he can tackle strongly and take the ball off an opposing attacker. Every team likes to have a creative midfield man, who can split opposing defences with a pass to his own forward, and there is always a demand for a left-sided player, to give the team the necessary balance and strength, since most footballers are right-footed. The left-sided player can increase the overall power of a team, and switch play around at the same time.

Because so much of the action during a game takes place in midfield, players whose job it is to win the ball and set up attacks for their own team cover every blade of grass, and this means that they must have plenty of stamina, for in addition to a defensive role, they must also be prepared to support their own forwards when the chance arises. Some players have the ability not only to get the ball, but they can go on powerful, surging runs

The side foot pass is made with the inside of the foot, keeping the body low and using the arms to ensure good balance. Once the pass has been made, the kicking foot continues to follow through.

The reverse pass is a good way of fooling an opponent. The player with the ball makes as if to go one way and while still maintaining that appearance makes the pass to the opposite direction, having 'sold' the move.

which take them past opponents, cut inside, and hammer in a drive which can sometimes bring a goal.

And when it comes to the three front men, there is a double job to be done, especially for a man playing wide on the wing. Not only does he have to try to beat a defender and get the ball across to the central strikers; he has to be prepared to go back and help his own defence when it's under pressure, and – having got possession – take the ball upfield and try to catch the opposition at sixes and sevens.

If the formation is 4-2-4, the front men must always be ready to give their team-mates in midfield a bit of help; if the formation is 4-4-2, the extra midfield man must be ready to reinforce the two attackers. But all the time, everyone has to be prepared to do something extra, in addition to his own job. Because, always remember, Soccer is a TEAM game, even if the formations vary from team to team.

Teamwork

There's an old Soccer saying that one man never made a team, and this is basically true. There may be one player in a side who is generally regarded as the star of the team; there may even be two or three players in one side who are rated as having exceptional ability. But it takes more than one player, or even two or three, to make things go right for a team throughout 90 minutes of play – even if a certain individual turns out to be the match-winner.

There was a time when Real Madrid had Puskas, Gento and di Stefano playing in the same side, and – not surprisingly – they were regarded by football fans as the stars. But while each player was always capable of scoring a spectacular goal that could win a game, the rest of the team helped to take Real through – and it is not always the man who gets goals that is the match-winner.

People still talk about a marvellous save Gordon Banks made for England against Pele in a World Cup-tie; they still remember how Alex Stepney denied the great Eusebio a goal when Manchester United played Benfica in the European Cup.

In the 1978 European Cup final at Wembley between Liverpool and F.C. Bruges, Dalglish scored the goal that won the trophy. It was the only goal of the game and, rightly, he was mobbed by his delighted team-mates. But it was a midfield player who spotted a narrow gap between defenders and pushed a 'slide-rule' pass through for Dalglish to take and chip the ball from the right into goal. His quick thinking made the scoring chance possible – that, and the accuracy of the pass.

So whether a team is defending or attacking, everyone has a part to play. An attacking move which brings a goal may have been started by the goalkeeper at the other end of the field. Picture the 'keeper throwing the ball out to his left-back, who

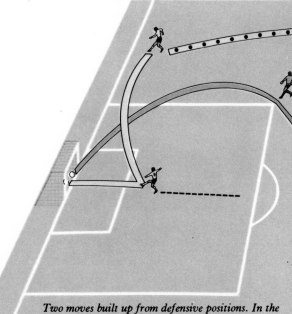

*Two moves built up from defensive positions. In the top move, (**A**) the goalkeeper passes the ball to the left back who passes it along the back line. The right back passes it to the midfield man who makes an attacking run down the right wing making a cross to the striker who shoots for goal.*

*The move down the left wing (**B**) starts with the left back making a run down the left wing, passing the ball to the midfield man. He runs into an attacking position before passing to the man just outside the penalty area who makes the shot for goal.*

*The long clearance from the goalkeeper (**E**) is aimed at the strikers, who run into the penalty area and shoot for goal.*

*In free kick (**F**) the kicker taps the ball to his team mate who runs in and shoots.*

*Going on a dummy run (**G**) when taking a free kick means that one of the players runs in as if he is about to take the kick, but runs over the ball while another player comes in to take the kick from a different angle.*

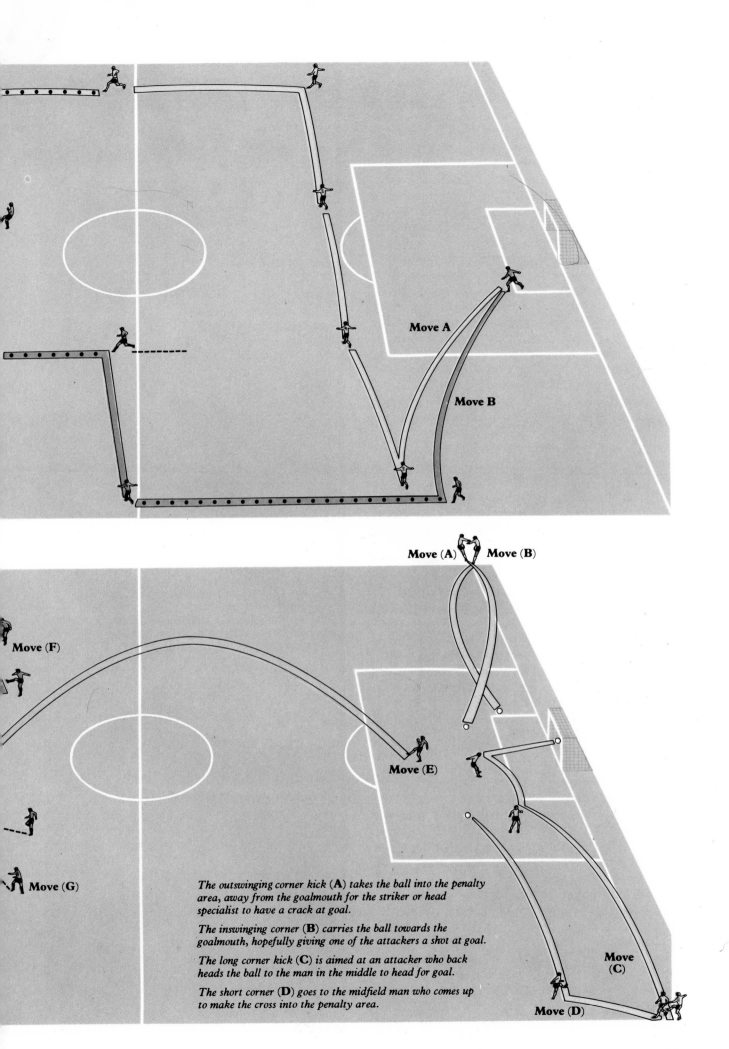

Move A

Move B

Move (A)   Move (B)

Move (F)

Move (E)

Move (G)

Move (C)

Move (D)

The outswinging corner kick (**A**) takes the ball into the penalty area, away from the goalmouth for the striker or head specialist to have a crack at goal.

The inswinging corner (**B**) carries the ball towards the goalmouth, hopefully giving one of the attackers a shot at goal.

The long corner kick (**C**) is aimed at an attacker who back heads the ball to the man in the middle to head for goal.

The short corner (**D**) goes to the midfield man who comes up to make the cross into the penalty area.

takes the ball forward to the half-way line, then slips it inside to a midfield man who has moved up into space. The midfield man takes the ball ten yards inside his opponents' half, pushes a pass through to one of the strikers, who hits a fierce drive from 20 yards and scores.

That's one example of the way an attack can be built up from the last line of defence – the goalkeeper. Another instance, with fewer moves, is when a 'keeper takes a long kick and the ball bounces into the opposition's 18-yard box, making it a battle between your strikers and one or both of the opposing central defenders to win possession.

Another example of building an attack from defence is when your team gains possession inside its own 18-yard box. The ball goes sideways from one back-four man to another, in short passing moves, then the last back-four man to receive the ball pushes it straight down the touchline to the winger ahead of him. The opposing side has been attacking, so they have pushed men upfield, leaving maybe one man lying back to guard against a breakaway. The winger gets the chance to take the ball upfield, commits the defender to move out towards him, while his team-mates try to chase back to cover. But one of your strikers is well on his way upfield, too . . . so the winger can leave the defender stranded by pushing a pass inside to the striker, who goes on for a shot, or the winger himself can get round the defender and cut inside to have a shot.

Naturally, teams practise moves during training and because players are aware of moves such as I have mentioned, they plan to counter them. So sometimes they can prevent a goal being scored from a breakaway, a long goal kick or an attacking move which has been built up from defence. That's where the teamwork comes into it, whether you're attacking or defending, and it's important for every player to be on the alert and make sure that, if possible, every gap is covered.

Again, at set-pieces (corners and free-kicks) teams practise moves which, they hope, will result in goals during games. A player taking a corner kick may give a certain signal which his team-mates will recognize, and they know that he plans to take an outswinger, which means he will send the ball over towards goal, but curling away from the goalkeeper. The idea is that as the 'keeper comes out in a desperate effort to connect with the ball and punch it clear, a striker will be able to move in and head the ball into goal.

A variation is the inswinger, where the ball curls in towards the goal, or the man taking the corner may send the ball straight and aim for a team-mate's head by the near post. The team-mate will then try to back-head the ball in the hope that someone on his side will be waiting to tuck it into the net. Then there is the short corner, where a player takes the kick and passes it to a team-mate a couple of yards away. He makes as if to cut inside

The player here makes the side foot volley look easy. His eye is firmly on the ball as it comes in to him. Balancing his body with his arms, he uses his left foot to make the pass and keeps his right foot firmly on the ground.

When making the chip pass the player runs directly at the ball, making a stabbing downward kick with little or no follow through.

past a defender – then he may switch the ball back to the player who took the corner, or push the ball across the face of goal for another team-mate to run in and try a shot.

When a free-kick is taken, perhaps 25 yards from goal, you often see one player shape as if to take the kick, then run over the ball, leaving it for a team-mate to follow up and hit the ball powerfully towards goal. Sometimes the first player will simply tap the ball a yard or two sideways, for a team-mate to hit it on the run; or maybe if it is a direct free-kick, where the kicker can score a goal, he will try to chip the ball over the defensive wall and over the goalkeeper, as well.

All these set-piece moves, and building up attacks from defensive situations, emphasize once again that it takes more than one man to win a game, in the long run; it takes teamwork and hard work to achieve success. It also takes brains, as well as brawn, because Soccer is a battle of wits, even though it is basically a simple game. When there are just 11 of you on a field, it's easy to pass the ball to each other without hindrance . . . but when there are 11 men against you, and 10 of them moving around trying to stop you from scoring, that's when you need to use your brains.

Goals

Think of 11 men linked together by an invisible string, and you begin to get the idea of how a football team works. There is the goalkeeper at the back, linked by separate strings to each of his four defenders . . . who are linked by more strings to three midfield men . . . who are linked yet again by those invisible strings to the three players up front. As one player moves around the pitch, and the invisible string moves with him, so the other players and strings move, making the 11 individuals join together as a team.

Of course, it is not always as simple as that, but the general idea is for every man in the side to be complementary to his team-mates, which means working together and for each other. This is team spirit in its best sense – unselfish play, willingness to help out – and when you have team spirit, you are half-way to success.

The goalkeeper may be in charge of his own area, but if he is firmly linked to the four men in the defensive line, while the midfield players supply the link between the back-four line and the men who play in the front line, you can build an attacking move from your own goalkeeper, via the back-four line and the midfield men; you can have the forwards dropping back to help out in defence when the opposition is pushing forward.

When the opposition is starting an attack – for instance, if their goalkeeper is about to take a kick – one or two of your own forwards drop back a bit deeper, hoping to intercept the kick or prevent the attackers making progress. Once your team has

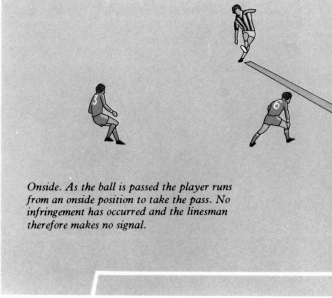

A player is in an offside position if, when a pass is made, there are not two defenders, including the goalkeeper, between him and the goal.

Offside. The player to whom the ball has been passed is standing in an offside position when the ball is passed. The linesman therefore signals for offside and a free kick is given to the defending side.

The offside trap. The defenders move forward as the ball is passed, leaving the receiver in an offside position. Again a free kick will be awarded.

Onside. As the ball is passed the player runs from an onside position to take the pass. No infringement has occurred and the linesman therefore makes no signal.

The wall pass. The player with the ball (above) being unable to pass the defender, passes the ball to his team mate (above left). He immediately returns the ball to the player who has now run round the defender (right) into position to take the return pass (far right). The wall pass is an effective way of getting a ball past a strong defender.

won the ball again, then you are in a position to start an attack of your own. And the ultimate object of the game is to score goals.

The team formations of today throw a great deal of weight upon the men who work in the front line, and often they find that they are outnumbered by the opposing defenders, so that scoring becomes more and more difficult. This is why it is essential that midfield players, or even defenders should add their weight to your attacks, and in recent years there has been an ever-increasing demand not only for goals, but for the goals to be spread around.

Most professional strikers – and their clubs – are satisfied if they wind up with 20 or more goals a season, which averages out at less than one a game, but this does mean that there is a demand for a scoring contribution from other players, notably midfield men.

Liverpool provide an excellent example of a team which spreads the goals around, for although in his first season Kenny Dalglish excelled, with a total of 31 goals in all competitions, the team as a whole totalled more than 100. Full-back Phil Neal scored seven goals, and Emlyn Hughes, Phil Thompson, Tommy Smith and Alan Hansen – all back-four men – also chipped in with goals. Twenty-nine goals came from midfield players, while forward David Fairclough contributed 15 goals.

Once again, it all goes to show that teamwork can pay off, in terms of the goals that win matches. It has to be admitted that some of the goals came from penalties, but they all count, and the fact that a team is awarded penalties shows, too, that they were in a good scoring position.

One tactic which some teams employ to make

sure the opposition does not get within striking distance is the operation of the offside trap. The offside trap may not be pretty to watch, and it can prove frustrating to players caught offside; but it is effective, although it can also be full of danger for the team operating the trap. Which means that you have to know exactly what you are doing, or you will be caught out yourselves, and leave the way wide open to the goal. Quite simply, the back-four line moves forward as a unit, to spring the offside trap – so you can see it is essential that each member of the unit is ready and alert, in order for the trap to succeed.

Beating the offside trap can be difficult, but it can be done, if the midfield men on the opposing team are geared for this, and their forwards are also poised for swift action. The trick is for the midfield man to push a pass through the advancing defence into the space behind them, and for a team-mate to make the break from a deep position at exactly the right moment, so that his speed takes him clear of the defenders and gives him the wide, open space with the ball, leaving the back-four men stranded.

One trick worth learning is coming in on the 'blind side' of the defence and poaching goals. This means that while play is going on at the right side of the field, say, around the edge of the 18-yard box, and the defenders are all concentrating on the player with the ball there, and those opponents nearest to them, there is a 'spare man' racing forward without the defenders realizing it (they do not have eyes in the backs of their heads) and when the player with the ball chips it over the defence and into the space behind them, the man moving forward has only the 'keeper to beat, usually from close range.

Another move which can pay dividends is the use of the 'early ball'. A player will move forward, taking the ball down the flank and then, instead of stopping and weighing things up before crossing the ball – that gives defenders time to weigh up the situation, as well – he will release the ball immediately, while still on the run, so that it goes behind defenders and gives a team-mate a chance to nip in and score.

So, you see, goals can come as a result of enterprising and thoughtful play by back-four men and midfield men, as well as forwards, and they can also tuck away scoring chances themselves. Indeed, the central defenders often get into the act at a set-piece such as a corner kick, when one of the two 'big fellows' goes upfield right into the opposition's goalmouth.

Of course, things can work the other way, as well, for while players are trying to score goals, other players – the opposing team – are trying to prevent them doing just that. Often you will see one team playing a 4-4-2 formation, with the two men up front as a twin spearhead. In that sort of situation, you may well see the two central defenders on the other side quickly sorting out what to do – one of them sticks with one striker, the other takes care of the second striker. And it is always easier to carry out the defensive part of the job than it is to be the striker, who often has his back to the goal as he tries to win the ball in the air.

In such circumstances, the striker will not even attempt to win the ball, then control it and turn to have a crack at goal. Instead, he will 'lay it off' – which means that he will concentrate on getting the first touch to the ball, with his head or maybe his chest, and immediately directing it towards his team-mate, who is already facing goal and may be in a good position to have a first-time shot at the target.

If the ball comes to a striker on the ground, while he has his back to the opposition's goal, it can be difficult to make good use of it when there's a hefty defender breathing down his neck. So again, the striker may 'lay it off' to a team-mate, then move away from the defender and hope to get a return pass, if his team-mate cannot get in a shot for goal. There are players who can take the ball on the ground, with their backs to goal and defenders right behind them, and then shield the ball from the defender before turning quickly and nipping round the defender while still in control of the ball.

But whatever the moves, whether they are aimed at scoring goals or preventing them, the accent remains on one thing – teamwork.

Incidentally, while people may talk about 'set-pieces' often being a waste of time, a survey has shown that something like 40 per cent of goals come from 'set-pieces'. As the glossary of Soccer terms tells you, a 'set-piece' is a move which is started from a static position – a free-kick, a corner kick, a throw-in and so on.

Right: The lofted drive is made by getting the foot directly under the ball and following straight through.

Left: The ball can be swung either in or out depending on which part of the foot is used. A produces an inswinger (see diagram) B makes the ball swing out.

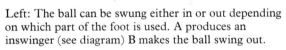

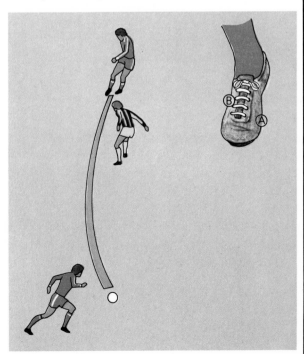

POSITIONAL PLAY

Goalkeeper

Goalkeepers may not be the glamour men of Soccer – but they are as important as any other players in the team. Once, clubs used to pay out only small fees for goalkeepers . . . but things have changed, and there is a general recognition today that a goalkeeper can save as many goals in a season as a forward can score. £300,000 has been paid for a goalkeeper and the team who paid it reckoned he was worth every penny as he made saves worth at least ten points to his team.

There are times when outfield players make mistakes, times when they 'hide' and take a breather. Most times, people forget or ignore the mistakes, because a team-mate is able to cover and come to the rescue. Often people do not realize an outfield player is 'hiding' . . . but let a goalkeeper lose his concentration and make a slip, and everyone is immediately aware. The goalkeeper is, perhaps, the loneliest man on the park; certainly the most vulnerable; and he is the man who cannot afford to make any mistake.

Some people used to say you had to be daft to be a goalkeeper. But the last line of defence in any team is far from being crazy. He has to be thinking a lot about the game, and on his toes all the time. Even when play is right at the other end of the field, he has to be weighing up the situation, because in a few seconds it can change, and he can be the man under pressure if the opposition breaks away and attacks. Especially if his own back-four men and midfield players have been left largely stranded upfield and he is on his own.

So concentration is one of the most important points for a 'keeper. If he is caught napping, he can look a fool – and nobody likes to feel a fool. A goalkeeper has to be agile and alert, because he has to cover a lot of ground in a matter of seconds. He may have to leap to catch the ball, dive at a forward's feet, throw himself to one side of goal or the other to deflect a scoring shot. Or he may have to stand there, body and hands braced to hold a shot which is coming at him at an incredible speed.

A goalkeeper has to be an acrobat and an athlete, physically brave to resist the challenge of a hefty striker, especially in the air. He has to be able to take off and catch the ball cleanly, even when it's almost parting the hair of a challenging forward. He needs good eyesight, too . . . and must be able to make instant decisions. When to stay on his line, when to come out for a ball, when to catch and when to punch clear. He also has to do a fair bit of talking during a game!

Bascially, he is the one man in his team who sees the whole of the play as it is going on in front of him, and this makes him the 'eyes' of the side. He must be in command of his own area, and be prepared to let his team-mates know that he is the man in charge. He must marshal the defence and call for the ball at the right time.

Above : When a corner is being taken the goalkeeper must try to ensure that he has both the kicker and the ball in view. If the corner kick is an inswinger as shown here, the 'keeper must be ready to come off his line and go up to meet the ball to gain possession.

Above : To narrow the angle, that is to give the attacker less space to aim his shot, the 'keeper moves out of his goal as the attacker approaches. The attacker has to decide which side of the 'keeper to aim his shot. If he goes for the narrow angle the 'keeper is naturally covering it, but he is ready to cover the wide angle if the shot is aimed there.

Above : A player taking a direct free kick is usually faced with a wall of defenders, who are effectively narrowing his angle. The 'keeper covers the exposed area of goalmouth, so the kicker will try to bend the ball round the wall, into goal out of the 'keeper's reach.

To take a ground shot, the 'keeper goes down with his body behind the ball, virtually collapsing on his left leg to get to the ground quicker. Once he has the ball he gathers it into his chest, making it impossible for the attackers to get at it.

Indeed, a goalkeeper can help to direct the defensive operations of his team, by making back-four players aware of the likely danger and the direction from which it can come. And all the time, he knows that, in the end, he is the very last line of defence himself.

When he plays against other teams, he sees forwards coming at him and he has to make up his mind, if one gets within shooting distance, how he can best narrow the angle – in other words, leave the forward the smallest possible gap at which to aim. He has to 'spread' himself at times, hoping that arms, legs or feet will stop the shot or deflect it to safety. In tight situations, such as when the ball comes over into a crowded goalmouth from a corner kick, he has to try to ensure that he is not crowded out by his own defenders or bundled off the ball by opponents striving to get it into the net. He can worry about the bruises later!

If you thought the goalkeeper's job was easy, or that he is more or less the man who makes up the number to 11, by now you will have realized that this is far from being the case. You may even be thinking of trying your luck as a goalkeeper yourself. If so, ask yourself if you measure up to the demands and requirements I have listed . . . and if the answer is yes, then good luck to you! One day you may become the sensation of the season.

You do not have to be a giant, but, obviously, height helps. So does the ability to take off and reach for the sky; and that agility I mentioned earlier. You need strength in your legs for kicking the ball, a safe pair of hands for catching cleanly . . . and that sixth sense which enables you to save certain scoring shots.

You can learn a lot by watching opposing forwards against whom you play regularly. Most of them have a 'favourite' foot for striking the ball, and they develop certain habits, because doing something a particular way comes naturally. When a player takes a penalty, for instance. He may try to blast the ball past you by sheer force, hoping that

even if you get a hand to the shot, the ball will still whizz past you. Or he may prefer to try to place the ball with an accurate kick. If so, study which side he likes to put the ball – at least, then, you have a chance of diving the right way.

You can study how players take corner kicks, and learn to cope with inswingers and outswingers, judging when to come off your line and when to stay. You can work out how to put a forward off, if it's between you and him – if he's got the ball and is racing for goal, you can advance and 'spread' yourself, so that he is caught in two minds about how to get the ball past you. But be careful you don't go out too far too soon, or you will be inviting him to chip the ball over your head and into goal!

Crosses, corners, penalties, strikers' techniques for scoring goals – these are all things a goalkeeper must cope with if he's going to succeed. He's also got to convince his own defenders that if he calls, they can safely leave things to him; and so the 'keeper gains command of his area, and the defenders are satisfied with things that way, because they trust their last line of defence.

Oh, yes – goalkeepers often make spectacular saves, but the best 'keepers are the ones who make the difficult saves look relatively easy. Every 'keeper lets in a 'soft one', now and again, but the best 'keepers are those who prove safe, rather than flashy, time and time again. The safe 'keeper is the man on whom his team-mates know they can rely.

Although the goalkeeper's position is basically a fixed one, there are times when, as I have said, he needs to come off his line, and this means that he needs speed off the mark over a short distance – indeed, he must be one of the fastest players in the team when it comes to sprinting short distances, so that if he spots a dangerous situation developing and he can see his defenders are likely to be caught out, he can race out of goal and get to the ball before the strikers, thus narrowing the angle.

The goalkeeper should also aim to be the best player in the side when it comes to kicking a 'dead' ball, and remember that kicking and placing of the ball (what is known as distribution) is very important. If you are taking a kick when the ball is 'dead', the whole idea is to make sure you find a team-mate with the kick. So kicking accurately is a vital part of the goalkeeper's job, and it is something which you should practise over and over again.

If play is at the other end of the field, that's the time when you should be ready to act as a 'sweeper' for your own defence, by coming out and standing around the penalty spot, ready for a sudden switch of play which may bring you into action. Some goalkeepers are willing to take the chance of running as far as 15 yards (13·5 metres) out of the penalty area and kicking the ball clear from a dangerous situation. Not long ago I saw a goalkeeper race out of his area to his left to deal with an attack. The ball was bouncing, and he and an opposing forward were racing to get to it. (Remember, because the 'keeper was out of his area he could not use his hands.) So what did he do? When he reached the ball first, he used his height to head it for a throw-in.

Generally speaking the goalkeeper is a ball-watcher, although he has to keep his eyes peeled for everything that is happening on the field. But while he is automatically noting which positions opposing players are taking up, he is still mainly concerned with where the ball is, and he has to be alert to make quick decisions – for instance, when the action is in his own area, he has to make up his mind whether he is going to catch the ball or punch it clear, especially when there are opposing players

Top and above: As the ball is crossed, the 'keeper dives in front of the attacker and punches it clear, using both his fists to do so. Punching a ball clear is quite an effective way of frustrating a shot at goal, but it is better if the 'keeper can make a clean catch.

Top and above: The 'keeper goes up for the ball, taking off on one foot and bringing the other up to give the jump more impetus. He watches the ball intently making sure that he is able to catch it cleanly, despite being fouled by the attacker who is leaning on him.

in close attendance. He has also got to keep a sharp eye on them!

Outfield players perhaps concentrate on developing leg muscles; a goalkeeper has to have a strong body, as well as strong leg muscles, to withstand charges from opponents and to cope with the speed of hard shots. So the basic rule is: always get your body behind the ball and, if at all possible, get both hands to the ball . . . relaxing as you catch it. Keep your eyes behind the flight of the ball for as long as possible, too – even when it's coming for your head. It is by no means easy to be so brave when you think a hard shot is liable to knock your head off your shoulders . . . but if you take your eye off the ball – and this can happen if you move your head out of the way ever so slightly – the next thing you know is that you have misjudged the situation and the ball has whistled past you and into the net.

So, from all this, you will realize that if a goalkeeper's job does not seem to have the same glamour as that of an outfield player, it is at least as important as that of any other man in the side. And if you find you have a real flair for catching and handling the ball, kicking well, judging how to stop it going into the net, then don't be afraid to step forward and say: 'I'll go in goal'. You may find that volunteering for this often unwanted position can pay dividends.

Full-back

Once upon a time, it was considered that a full-back had done his job by simply being there to prevent the opposing winger from getting past him. But not any more. Playing at full-back today means that you have to defend when necessary, and be prepared to support your team in attack whenever the chance presents itself. And it has always got to be remembered that when two teams are in opposition, gaining possession of the ball is vital, because the team that has the ball is the one with the initiative. The side without the ball is the one which is on the defensive.

In years gone by, the full-back was looked upon as a player with limited skills. He was strong, and he might or might not be fast. But when he went into a tackle, his opponent was left in no doubt about it! The full-back showed his strength, also, in the way he could give the ball the 'big boot' – clearing it up the field. But again, sometimes he did not always use the ball to the best advantage of his side, for when he whacked it, it might go straight to an opponent . . . and so his side was immediately on the defensive again.

Today, the full-back is often an all-purpose player, in the sense that he is not only a defender, but a player capable of making attacking moves himself. He has to be able to move quickly, and to think quickly, whether it's sizing up how to rob an opponent of the ball or how to go forward himself

51

on the overlap and help to put the opposition under pressure. Some full-backs even feature on the score sheet!

So you can see that the job of playing at full-back is not simply a matter of standing there and waiting to win the ball from or whack an opposing winger. Obviously, a full-back relies a great deal on his ability to intercept and tackle when he makes a challenge aimed at winning the ball, and again, he can use his defensive powers in one of two ways. He can stay very close to a winger, marking him tightly so that the winger gets no time or room to control the ball, or he can concern himself with what is termed zonal defence.

When the marking is tight, it means that the full-back sticks close to his direct opponent – and, indeed, other players in the side may be close-marking other opponents in a similar way. However, if the full-back is figuring in a system which involves zonal marking, it means that, like the other rear defenders, he covers a certain area of the pitch and this means that any player who comes into that area becomes his immediate concern.

There are times when you can allow an opponent to play around with the ball, so long as he is not making progress – but the closer opponents get to your goal, the tighter must be the marking. And if a winger gets the ball so that he is able to go down the flank at speed, the full-back then has to be careful to avoid committing himself with a rash tackle . . . or he will find the winger skipping past him with the ball and leaving him trailing. That's when a full-back can jockey the winger, keeping him covered but not rushing in to intercept. So the winger has to slow down.

In such a situation, the full-back takes care to stay on the inside of the winger, watching his every move while keeping just a few feet away. This means that the winger has greater trouble going past the back on the outside, or cutting inside; for the defender is ready to make his tackle then whichever way the winger decides to go. By jockeying the winger, too, the back is giving his fellow-defenders time to cover, so that if he is finally beaten, a team-mate can try to stop the attacker – or, if the back is fast enough and confident of his ability to turn quickly, he can make a second attempt to stop the winger going on, cutting inside or crossing the ball.

The full-back also has certain responsibilities to his goalkeeper – indeed, all the players in the back-four line have – for while the 'keeper may be the boss in his own area, and do the calling to marshal his defence, there are times when he has to come right out and try to take a high ball. This means that as he commits himself to coming out, he is bound to leave the goal behind him exposed, and if he makes a mistake and does not get the ball, an opposing forward who has been on the alert, can nip in and slot the ball into the net. So when the 'keeper comes out to take the ball high, one or two

of the back-four men know they need to give him cover on the goal line itself. Then, if there is any slip-up, and a forward tries a header or a shot, a defender stands a chance of clearing the ball right off the line.

Even when a full-back is beaten by a forward, there is still a job for him to do, because he can at least retreat towards his own goal in such a way that he gives as much protection as possible in another direction. Once he has been beaten out on the wing, and realizes he will not get a second chance, the full-back will make for the near post, so that he can stand a chance of cutting out the danger whether the winger crosses the ball or cuts inside with it himself. And always the back-four line as a whole is working as a unit, ready to help out and try to get its own midfield players and forwards on the attack.

Time and again, a team which is under pressure can suddenly become the attackers, if everyone in

On being challenged by a defender, the player with the ball taps it through his opponent's legs and runs round him to regain possession. This move is known as 'nutmegging'.

the side is thinking and working to this end. Again, it boils down to the two essentials of teamwork and making sure that your side gains possession. Because once you have done that, the opposition has some hard and quick thinking to do.

And when you sum up the function of the modern full-back, it is fair to say that he must be an all-round player in the team. His job is not just to stop people and give the ball the 'big boot' – it is to tackle, mark men, be a good header of the ball and a strong runner over distances of more than 50 yards – remember, when he makes a run upfield, he also has to be able to get back and resume his defensive role in the game.

He must also be a good striker and passer of the ball, and have good control of it. Indeed, he must be the all-round player in the side, and have many of the qualities we look for in players who occupy other positions.

Central Defenders

In the days of the old W-M formation, the man with the No. 5 on his jersey was THE centre-half, or pivot. Now there are two centre-halves in each team, although we refer to them as central defenders.

Many professional central defenders say that they are helped in their defensive jobs because at one time they operated as strikers, so they learned from playing a role up front how forwards try to get the better of back-four men. Other players may have played midfield before dropping back to their present positions in the side. And some people will say that it is easier to drop back, once you have played in another position further forward in the team. Certainly every bit of experience helps you to become a more complete footballer.

At one time, the old centre-half – the centre-half

who wore the No. 5 shirt – was regarded purely as a 'stopper'. It was his job simply to prevent the opposing centre-forward getting within sight of goal. But with twin strikers operating these days, the two central defenders have come more and more to the forefront. And if you play as a central defender, it certainly helps if you are tall, because one of the essential qualities you need is the ability to get up for the ball in the air . . . and to win it.

Watch any football match, and you will often see the ball kicked in the air towards the twin strikers. It may be a long, high cross from the flank, or it may be a ball out of defence aimed more or less directly down the centre of the field, towards those twin strikers. Like the central defenders, they are expected to be good in the air, too – but the central defenders usually have one great advantage. When a high ball comes into the 18-yard box or there-abouts, the defenders are facing the right way for it, while the strikers often have to challenge for the ball while they have their backs to goal. So the advantage is with the central defenders.

Often, also, you will see (if you look closely enough) that one of the central defenders is keeping a close watch on a particular striker, while the other central defender marks the striking 'twin'.

That long, high ball which is crossed into the 18-yard box is commonly used to try to put the central defenders under pressure, and you will see one of the strikers going up with the man marking him. The striker will be trying to get his head to the ball first, and direct it towards his 'twin', hoping that he can control it on the ground, get past his opponent, and shoot for goal. By the same token, when a central defender goes up for the ball, his aim is to beat the striker to it and, if possible, head the ball to a team-mate.

But sometimes, especially if there are a lot of players milling around in the penalty area, the defender does not have time or room to ensure that he gets the ball to a team-mate . . . in which case, that 'safety-first' motto is applied, as the central defender simply heads the ball as powerfully as he can, and as high and as far away from the danger area as possible. There are times when a central defender tries to be too clever – either on the ground or in the air – and he attempts to play his way out of trouble. The problem is that too often, because he has not been decisive enough, he plays his own team into trouble, since he has made almost a gift of the ball to the opposition.

So it is vital for a central defender to make up his mind what he is going to do, to move quickly to the ball and play it early, instead of dithering or trying to do the elegant thing. What looks good is not always the most effective method of dealing with a tight situation. If you fiddle about with the ball, trying to show the opposition how clever you are, you will get no thanks from your team-mates especially if your extravagent dillying and dallying produces a goal for your opponents.

Below: To make a feint, the attacker approaches the challenger making as if to go to the left. He switches direction, going to the right, making enough room to set himself up for a shot.

Below: To 'turn' an opponent, as the ball comes through to the player he takes it on his right foot, pulls it to his left and flicks it so that it turns round his opponent, giving him a clear shot at goal.

There is an art in winning the ball in the air, too; it is not just a matter of being six feet tall and getting your feet off the ground. You have to learn to flex your muscles so that you get the maximum 'take-off' when you go up for the ball, because the chances are that your opponent will be as tall as yourself. You need to time your jump so that you do not get to the top of your leap too soon and miss the ball – and you have to time it so that you are not too late in arriving. And all the time, keep your eye on the ball, as they say in golf. Watch it until you get it right on your forehead. Incidentally, it is not just the ability to leap like a salmon that's required; you need to use your neck muscles so that you gain maximum power to direct the ball away to safety.

A bouncing ball can be a problem for a central defender, especially if he is under pressure. I once saw a match in which a defender went up to head the ball, while two opponents were also challenging for possession. The defender, instead of concentrating on getting the ball in the air, had his attention distracted to some extent by the challengers. He mistimed his jump and missed the ball completely. Neither of the opposing forwards got the ball, either – but when it bounced awkwardly, it caught the defender's hand and the result was that the opposition were awarded a penalty. And they scored.

What about the ball when it's on or fairly close to the ground? Again, a central defender has to have a good pair of feet, because he must be able to get the ball away in a hurry, and he is not always given time to take it on his favourite foot. He cannot afford to wait for the ball to finish bobbing around, either, so often he has to kick it before it touches the ground. If you let the ball start bobbing around you, you are asking for trouble. You can hit the ball on the volley and get it clear if you read the situation correctly.

Obviously, a central defender must possess the ability to tackle and intercept, as well as kick the ball away. And, as is the case with the full-back dealing with a winger, the central defender cannot afford to commit himself rashly. He has to time his tackle correctly. His best plan is to make the attacker keep the ball in front of him, denying him the chance to play it past the defender. This not only gives the defender a bit of time to make his own challenge; it allows team-mates to cover should anything go wrong.

Basically, the central defender is concerned with preventing attacks getting through to goal, whether in the air or on the ground. But he has never to forget that, although he is a defender, he can set his own attack in motion, by a shrewd clearance aimed directly at one of his team-mates; or into a space where a team-mate can gain possession. So accuracy in kicking, as well as power and distance, is an important part of a central defender's game.

While the accent may be on defence, so far as he is concerned, there are times when he can turn

As the man in possession is challenged for the ball, he takes the ball onto his outside foot and puts his body between the challenger and the ball. He is effectively screening the ball.

Bottom left: the correct way to take a throw in. Below centre: a foul throw in. Below right: the position for taking a long throw in.

Above, top left and left: The low drive is made by approaching the ball directly using a long stride, connecting with the ball and following through with real power.

Right: As a high ball approaches, the player pivots on the ground leg and swings his kicking leg at the ball to make a side volley. Balance is maintained by using the arms as shown here.

himself into an extremely useful attacker, by seizing on any offensive chance that presents itself.

One final point: while there are two central defenders, it is usually the job of one of them to take charge of the back-four line as a unit, talking to his team-mates and marshalling them so that they do their defensive job as effectively as possible. Just as a goalkeeper does his share of talking and 'calling' during a match, so the central defender who is in charge of the back-four division gives a lead, and often you will see that it is one of the central defenders who is captain of the side, although sometimes a midfield player is the skipper.

Midfield

The midfield player is arguably the busiest man in the team during a match, for he combines two jobs in one. When necessary, he has to support the attack; and when his own side is under pressure, he has to be prepared – and able – to give a helping hand (or, rather, foot) in defence. There is an old saying that the team which controls the middle of the field will probably win the game, and while this may not be 100 per cent correct, certainly the team which controls midfield is odds-on to control the way the game goes.

Every top midfield player in football has one thing in common, even if they vary in individual skills or special qualities. This is that the midfield man gets involved in the game, right the way through the 90 minutes. So he is, arguably, the busiest man in the side. Some midfield players are what is known as ball-winners, which means that as well as having the basic skills, they are strong enough physically to go into the tackle against an opponent and come out with the ball. Other players have more delicate skills to offer as their contribution to the team effort, for they may specialize in the art of precise passing, over long or short distances, and supplying forwards with the sort of ball which gives them a clear opening for the opposition's goal.

The function of a midfield man is many-sided: he must be able to prompt attacks (and join in them), yet recognize when he needs to concentrate on a defensive role, especially in intercepting the ball to stop the opposition mounting an attack.

The midfield player is constantly in the thick of the action, and because he has such a variety of jobs to do, he needs stamina, speed, quickness of thought, accuracy in passing, vision in being able to 'read' situations and create space for himself and team-mates, and generally have more than a little of every quality that goes to make up the complete footballer.

Not surprisingly, most youngsters fancy that

Liam Brady of Arsenal dribbles the ball upfield. As the challenger comes in, Brady has given himself enough room to make an effective pass by screening the ball from the opponent who can only give chase.

they are cut out to be midfield players . . . but remember that this is not always the case; and remember, also, that if you fail to make a hit as a midfield man, you can still stand a chance of making your mark in another position.

For a defender in the back-four line, height is an important consideration, but when it comes to playing in midfield, you do not have to be a giant. There are some tallish midfield international players, but other top players are the living proof that so long as you have what it takes, you can play a starring role as a midfield man, and the big consideration is your all-round ability. For all-round play is the midfield man's strong suit.

He must be able to win or receive the ball, know when and where to pass the ball, for the best advantage of his team. He must also have the ability to spot an opening for himself, so that he can break forward and get clear of defenders to take a pass and set himself up for a scoring chance. Needless to say, he must finally have the ability to stick the ball into the net when he gets that chance.

Usually, two of the midfield players combine to set up and join in the attacking moves when their team is able to push forward, with the third midfield man (if it's a 4-3-3 formation) staying back to act as an 'anchor' man. He will be the ball-winner in the midfield department, more often than not, but the other two midfield players must never forget their defensive duties, either, so that if an attack does break down, they must quickly get back to cover opponents and generally help out while their team is on the defensive.

A lot can be said for a midfield player, because he really is involved in just about everything that happens on the field during a game. He is part of the team's 'engine room', with his workload of attacking, defending, passing, putting his own forwards on the attack, breaking through to join in attacks himself and so on. And more and more, teams are relying on midfield players adding to the total contribution of goals, for with the two central strikers so often being tightly marked by the opposing central defenders, it's the midfield men who can get free into space to create danger in the opposition's goalmouth.

It's impossible for any player to guarantee to score a certain number of goals during a season, but while it is reckoned that a professional striker is doing well if he maintains a scoring rate of 20 goals a season, any midfield player worth his salt will be aiming to get into double figures as a marksman.

To sum up, then, the midfield man needs plenty of stamina to cover a tremendous amount of ground during a game. He is the link man between defence and attack, so he needs to make sure he's never far from where the action is. He must be able to control the ball well, shield it when he is under challenge, and turn quickly to get away from his challenger. He must be a good 'reader' of the way things are going in a game, be ready to intercept, to

make passes which can throw the opposition off balance, and always be prepared to push forward in support of his own strikers, so that if they are under pressure, they can lay the ball off so that it is in just the right position for the midfield player when he is breaking forward.

Stamina, skill, all-round ability in the air and when tackling, passing over short or long distances, and shooting . . . these qualities are the trademark of the good midfield player. In short, he must have the ability to make the difficult things look easy.

Wingers

England won the World Cup in 1966, it was said, without wingers, and it took 10 years for them to come back 'into fashion'. The plain fact is that, although Soccer tactics have changed over the years, there has always been room for the footballer who could play on the flank and give a team what is known as 'width' – in other words, someone to operate in a wide position and provide the ammunition for the central strikers.

Years ago, England had in Tom Finney a player who could operate equally well on the left wing, on the right wing, at inside-forward or centre-forward. There was also Stanley Matthews, whose speciality was right-wing play. He would leave defenders flat-footed and sometimes sprawling on the ground as he dribbled round them in a manner which appeared to make them hazy. The great Real Madrid team which monopolized the European Cup in its early days had Gento – he played in 94 European ties, more than any other European footballer – and the Hungarians who shattered England by winning 6–3 at Wembley had Ferenc Puskas, the 'galloping major' whose left foot could cause more havoc than many other players could achieve with two good feet.

Today, Real Madrid have a Danish winger, Henning Jensen, who cost them around £300,000; and another Danish wing star, Allan Simonsen, who played for Borussia Moenchengladbach against Liverpool in the 1977 European Cup final in Rome, won the vote as European Footballer of the Year. At the end of the 1978 season in the North American Soccer League, Dennis Tueart – who scored two goals for New York Cosmos in the final play-off victory over Tampa Bay Rowdies – was voted the 'most valuable player'.

Speed, ball control, the ability to beat a defender and the powerful shot – these are the attributes of the successful winger. Entertainment value is added as a bonus – and whenever a class winger gets the ball, you can be sure the crowd will start to tingle with a sense of anticipation, because they feel that he is likely to produce something a bit special.

It's worth remembering, too, that good wingers should possess the ability to crack the ball hard when they get a sight of goal. This is an extra asset, because it aids striking power to the front line as

A long range shot from 25 yards out is made by using the lofted drive (see page 43). By hitting one side of the ball, using the instep at the moment of contact, keeping the head over the ball and following through, it swerves away from the 'keeper into the net.

Left: The correct way to take a penalty. By running directly at the ball, the kicker gives the 'keeper no indication as to what side he intends to aim the ball. By the time the ball has left the player's foot, it is usually too late for the 'keeper to make a clean save.

Right: The wrong way to take a penalty. By running in at an angle, the kicker has given the 'keeper some indication as to what side he is going to go for.

well as the ability to get round a defence on the outside or open it up by cutting the ball back into the area. A winger is expected to be able to supply accurate, high crosses for the central strikers, but it is not always the most effective way of causing trouble for the opposition. A winger who can get round the full back and go to the goal line, then turn inward and cut the ball back towards his own strikers, low across goal, offers something which threatens danger from a totally different direction.

It is sometimes the job of a midfield player to take corner kicks, because of his ability to place the ball precisely from a static situation, but often it is the winger who is responsible for taking corners – perhaps from either flank – and he must know how to make the ball curl inwards towards goal, or take an outswinger which can evade the 'keeper and, hopefully, the defenders. Sometimes you will see the winger take a short corner, passing the ball only a few yards to a team-mate, who then has the option of cutting inside with the ball himself, slipping it square for a third team-mate or pushing it back to the winger, who will then have a few yards of space in which to manoeuvre and get round the nearby defenders.

The winger can also profit from being able to drive the ball hard across goal, for sometimes this brings a goal. It needs only a touch from a striker – or an unfortunate deflection from a defender trying desperately to clear – for the ball to be turned goalwards and, at the speed with which the ball is travelling, it will go like a rocket towards the target area.

The winger is primarily an attacking player, of course, and his team-mates rely on him to break clear of defences and set up attacks from the flank, in various ways. However, in the modern game the winger must always be prepared to do a defensive job when his team has lost the initiative. For instance, if the opposing 'keeper is taking a goal kick, you will find the winger dropping back to help his own midfield men cover every situation.

If the 'keeper looks as if he might throw the ball out to a full-back, the winger will close up on the full-back so that the 'keeper, more than likely, will not risk the ball being lost to the other team. And if the winger's team is under pressure, or the opposing full-back makes an attacking foray down the flank, the winger will fall back to mark him and try to gain possession.

In the same way, when the opposition is taking a corner kick, the winger of the defending side will go back to 'pick up' an opponent – and always the winger will be ready and alert for the chance to get the ball and make an attacking break himself. So he patrols one flank or the other, ready to act as an extra defender when required and to get the ball upfield and provide the ammunition for his own team to turn defence into speedy attack.

A winger who gains possession of the ball in space starts off with a tremendous advantage,

Below: As a lofted ball comes in, the player tenses his body ready to jump up, with his body and neck arched, to head the ball clear.

Below: The ball comes across the goal, and, keeping his eyes fixed on it, the attacker makes a leaping header, getting up over the ball so that he can head it downwards, hopefully into goal.

Above, top right and right:
The defender, in the striped
shirt makes the defensive
header by getting in front of
the attacker and timing his
jump so that he is higher in
the air as the ball comes
over. The secret of
successful heading is to keep
the eyes firmly on the ball as
it approaches.

Above left, left and far left:
The backward header is
made by taking the impact
of the ball on top of the
head and nodding the ball
backwards.

because he is then able to work up speed, and once he is in full flight, he looks great as he speeds past a full-back. Obviously, it is important for a winger to be able to dribble, and beat an opponent by using not only his speed, but his ability to control the ball while moving forward. But it is equally important for the winger to know when to take on a defender and when he is in a position to use the ball to better advantage by making a pass to a team-mate. In order to beat your man, even when you are going at full speed, you have to use that speed to get past him on the outside. Or, if he proves that he is as fast as you are, you must use your change of pace and body swerve to cut inside him, or deceive him by suddenly pulling up, and switching the ball to a team-mate.

A change of pace and direction can be as effective as beating a man by sheer speed or dribbling round him or slipping the ball between his legs. And one thing is sure – never try to be too clever. If you dribble round an opponent, do not stand back and admire your own handiwork; having done the hard bit, you would be foolish to give him another chance to get possession. Make sure that, having beaten him, you make further progress, possibly drawing other defenders towards you and so creating space for your fellow-forwards, who can really benefit from your pass if it is made at the right time.

If a defender is marking you closely when you have the ball, try a body swerve, so that you can make to go one way, then swiftly go to the other. And when you are taking a corner kick, make sure that you can reach the target area, while keeping the ball away from the 'keeper. Drop the ball short of the 'keeper, play it beyond him, or – if you are kicking into the goal area – use the outswinger or inswinger to cause him problems.

With the outswinger, you can tantalize the goalkeeper by making him leave his line, yet kicking the ball in such a way that it still curls out of his reach. Remember, by coming out and going up in the air, he has left his goal exposed, and that gives your strikers the chance of an opening. If you take an inswinger, make sure the ball curls close in so that the 'keeper is committed to going for it – remembering again that as he does this, he will be under challenge from your strikers at a time when he is vulnerable, because he's going through the air and must rely on his judgment in catching the ball or punching clear.

When a winger takes an inswinging corner, the 'keeper must have one eye on the opposing striker or strikers, so it is difficult for him to concentrate 100 per cent on getting the ball away. And, as a matter of interest, do not forget that a throw-in from near the corner flag can be as good as a corner

The front block tackle. The player on the right is in possession and the tackler comes in, going forward with his weight over the ball. Bending his knees to achieve the proper balance, he comes away cleanly with the ball.

to the attacking side, provided they have a player who can reach the goalmouth with a long throw.

In short, the winger may not be the complete footballer that the midfield man is expected to be, but he has at his disposal a range of tricks which bear his own special stamp and add not only excitement and entertainment to the game, but provide that ammunition for scoring goals.

One of the important aspects of wing play is knowing where and when to dribble. Don't try to dribble round an opponent and risk giving the ball away so that it puts your own defence in trouble. Don't try your tricks in the wrong places – such as your own half of the field. Wait until you are in his half of the field. Unless you have the space to go forward with the ball in your own half, play the ball back to a defender, then move up to get a return pass from a team-mate.

The winger must have, and be prepared to use, a quick change of pace. When he is running at a full-back with the ball, he must keep the ball within playing distance, so that he is in control. And whether he beats the back on the inside or the outside, no matter how many times the winger feints before he makes his move, the trick is to push the ball a few yards past the back, then quickly change the pace to get past him. By pushing the ball past the back, the winger has made him turn, and

with a quick burst of speed the winger should get two yards clear of the back. The winger then accelerates even more to get clean away.

Do not try to push the ball across the back, otherwise he gets the chance to turn and confront you again. Make the back do something positive by committing himself so that if he does get within distance of you or the ball he gives away a corner, a throw-in or even fouls you. Try to ctach him when he's off balance, as you go past him. If he has all his weight on one foot, that's when you knock the ball past him, keeping it a couple of yards from him so that he is unable to stick out a foot and deflect the ball to safety. Practise ball control with both feet while you're running. Use both the inside and outside of the feet to control the ball. And practise quick turns by putting your foot on the ball, and in the same movement, turning and moving off in another direction.

One of the hardest things for a winger is to make an accurate cross while on the run. This means that after you have beaten the full-back and broken clear, you are crossing the ball at right angles into the centre of the field, so you are kicking the ball across your own body.

Of course, you have to be able to shoot, so that you can make your contribution to the team effort by way of goals.

The side block tackle. The tackler comes in from the side, turning as he goes in for the ball and effectively blocking the man in possession.

Strikers

Every time a game of football is played, the object is for one team to finish up by scoring more goals than the opposition. That may seem to be stating the obvious, and sometimes, perhaps, if you are playing against a very defensive team, you may be tempted to wonder if goals are what the game is all about! But generally speaking, the big idea is to get the ball into the net, and this brings us to the players who have the direct responsibility for doing just this. The strikers.

You will hear people saying that strikers hunt in pairs, and there are many examples of this. But whether this is true or not, they all have one thing in common, a hunger for goals and the ability to get the ball into the net, whether with the head or with the foot.

One of the most effective strikers, Johan Cruyff will drift around almost like a ghost, appearing unexpectedly on one side of the field or the other, and then suddenly materializing inside the 18-yard box to get on the end of an attacking move and finish it off with a goal.

Uwe Seeler and Gerd Mueller, who scored so

many goals for their clubs and for West Germany, are good examples of strikers. Mueller, like Seeler before him, is powerfully built and strikes directly for the target. Eusebio, who played for Portugal in the 1966 World Cup in England – and scored four goals in one game against North Korea – was tall, lithe and sinewy, which meant that he could deceive opponents and set himself up for the shot, and West Brom today have a player who, perhaps, resembles Eusebio in many respects . . . Cyrille Regis, the coloured youngster who seems destined to wear the international jersey of England before he has finished. Regis is so fast off the mark he can speed past defenders even though he has given them a start, and he rifles shots past goalkeepers with great accuracy.

If the midfield player is primarily the maker of chances and the creator of attacks, the striker is the taker of chances and the man in the firing line. And as such, he has to be prepared to take plenty of 'stick' inside the 18-yard box, because defenders quickly come to recognize a dangerous opponent, and they don't stand on ceremony!

Denis Law was one of the greatest strikers in post-war years, and I've heard it said that he would

go in where angels feared to tread. In other words, he was prepared to go in where it really hurt – inside that 18-yard box – and take everything the big defenders could dish out. His answer to them all was quite simple . . . leave the ball in the back of the net.

Certainly the striker must be ready to chase and fight for the ball every inch of the way, and because there is so much physical contact, he must not be lacking in courage. He has to face the fact that, often, he will have his back to goal when the ball comes to him, while the big, burly defender is breathing down his neck. He has to accept that when he's going forward, a defender will be there, prepared to put in a crunching tackle. He has to be prepared, also, to be out-numbered inside the area, especially when he has the ball and is running at defences.

So courage is high on the list of qualities a striker must possess. And courage is not merely physical, for a striker's job, in the end, is to get the ball past the goalkeeper – which means that, if he gets even half an opening, he must believe in himself sufficiently to be ready to hit the ball with head or foot straight at the target. If a striker gets an opening,

and decides to pass the ball square to a team-mate, it may be because he thinks the team-mate will have a better chance of scoring; or it may be that he is ducking his own responsibility, because he has not got that belief in himself to score.

At times, it may seem that a goal is out of the question, because the angle left to the striker is so narrow. But if he gets a sight of goal, it's up to him to have a go, if he really feels he can beat the 'keeper.

When strikers go hunting in pairs, they work on a very real understanding with each other, so that one man knows almost by telepathy what his partner can or will do, in certain situations. For instance, if the ball is played down the centre and in the air to the 'target man' – the player who can get up high for the ball – his partner will be lurking close by as the big fellow goes up to make contact with the ball. The partner knows that his team-mate will try his utmost to direct the ball – with head or maybe chest – downward into his path, so that he can have a crack at goal.

If the ball comes to one of the 'twins' on the ground, and he has his back to goal with a defender in close attendance, the partner will move into

The slide tackle. The man in possession seems to have got round his man, but the tackler makes a successful side tackle by making contact with the ball with his left leg, bringing his right knee in front of the other player's leg. No foul has been committed as he was going for the ball, not the man.

position again, a few yards away, ready to take a quick pass and set himself up for a shot. So you will see from this that the goals scored by strikers hunting in pairs can come from deliberate actions, and are not just the result of lucky accidents.

Even so, the majority of goals do come as a result of defensive errors, and the striker must always remember this. So all the time, he has to believe that if he does his job properly, and runs and chases and fights for the ball, he can cash in on a defender finally making a mistake in judgment. He may persuade the defender to commit himself to a tackle too soon, or he may shield the ball from the defender then suddenly turn and break clear.

And when the chance comes to get in the shot, the striker must have the conviction that he can score. Because the goalkeeper, too, is capable of making a mistake. Even the best of 'keepers lets in a goal unexpectedly, by letting the ball slip through his arms or under his body. Occasionally, indeed, the 'keeper may be fooled when a striker has a go for goal, because the ball may look as if it is curling over the bar or just wide of a post . . . then dip and go past the 'keeper into the net.

The primary job of the striker is to get into a position where, on receiving the ball, he is in with a chance of scoring a goal. No matter whether he is outnumbered, or whether the chance is a slim one at most, he must be alert and ready to shoot or head for the target, because the opening can appear suddenly and often unexpectedly. It's happened before that even when a defender looks to have won the ball, he slices a clearance so that it goes to a player of the opposing side. And at the end of the day, the law of averages will apply. If you put in enough goalbound shots or headers, the chances are that SOME of them will count. So for a striker, it's vital that he should shoot at every opportunity.

Practising shooting (and taking penalties) is a 'must' for a striker, because it is essential that not only does he get in as many shots and headers as possible – they've got to be accurate. Hard low drives to the corner are the ones most likely to beat a 'keeper, but strikers can also benefit from deflections in a crowded goalmouth, so that the 'keeper is left stranded by the ball which suddenly moves away from him. The main thing, then, is to practise shooting and heading, and make sure you remember to maintain this during a game, because as a striker, goals are your business. And any striker will tell you that every goal is a good one, no matter whether it came about as he intended or as a result of a liberal helping of luck.

Summing up, a striker should be good in the air, either to flick the ball on, lay it off or head for goal. He needs to be strong, to withstand a hard challenge, and, especially if he isn't tall, very fast over short distances. A striker needs to pack a shot in either foot, be able to lay the ball off first time, and to screen it, have good ball control, especially with his back to goal – and be ready to shoot quickly.

The man in the middle – the referee – is the man whose decision is final, and players should always remember this. Linesmen are there to assist and be available for consultation, but the referee can over-rule a linesman, so he still has the last word.

The referee and linesmen are easily identified by their distinctive black uniforms, and there are certain important items of equipment which the referee should always check before he takes charge of a game. He must make sure he arrives at a ground in good time, and he must inspect the pitch and the match equipment, so that everything is in order before the game begins.

Apart from his own uniform, the referee has to make sure that he has his personal items of equipment – two watches, one of them having a 'stop' action so that he can add the necessary time for stoppages of play; two whistles – if possible, differing in tone; two pencils, a note pad and/or a scorecard; a coin; and a copy of the rules of the competiton covering the game he is refereeing and a referees' chart.

The referee can caution a player, or send him off, and he also has the power to report officials and spectators who interfere with the progress of the match. In the case of a player who is injured, the referee can allow the trainer on the field, or order that the player should be removed from the field of play and over the touchline for treatment. The referee must also know the laws of the game (and show this, by having passed an examination) and he must be of the required standard of fitness, which means that before the season begins, he takes a fitness test.

Usually, before he is promoted to the League list of referees, he has served a considerable time in the lower grades of Soccer, gradually working his way up the ladder. When he becomes a League referee, he receives payment and expenses for doing the job, and if he makes a success of being a referee, he will stay on the list until he reaches the compulsory retirement age of 47. Naturally, he hopes that he will prove good enough to be appointed to officiate at an FA Cup final or League Cup final, and to get on to the FIFA panel of referees, which means he is qualified to handle international matches.

While the referee is the man whose decision is final, it is not his job to draw attention to himself – rather, his job is to control a match efficiently and unobtrusively, so that play is allowed to flow while, at the same time, he is in real command. Players often say it's a sign that it was a good game because they never noticed the referee!

A good referee always tries to prevent confusion regarding his decisions and, with this in mind, he has a series of signals which he can use to indicate why he gave a certain award. The diagrams here illustrate signals used by a referee so that fans and players alike can immediately see what the referee has awarded, and why.

For instance, at a free-kick the referee will

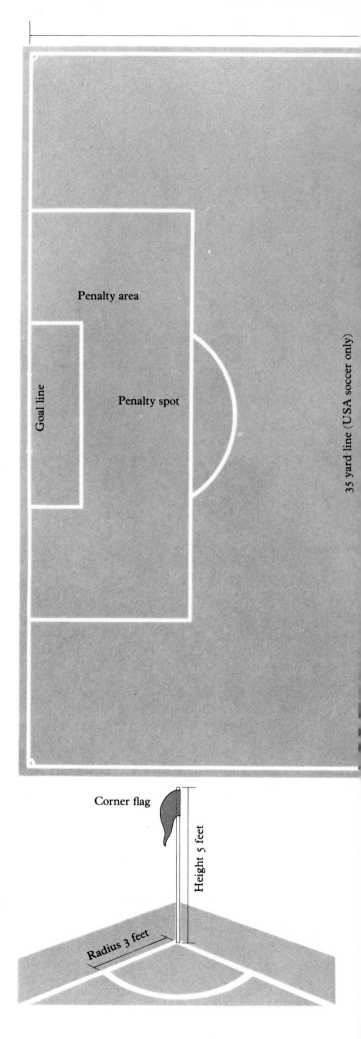

Penalty area

Goal line

Penalty spot

35 yard line (USA soccer only)

Corner flag

Height 5 feet

Radius 3 feet

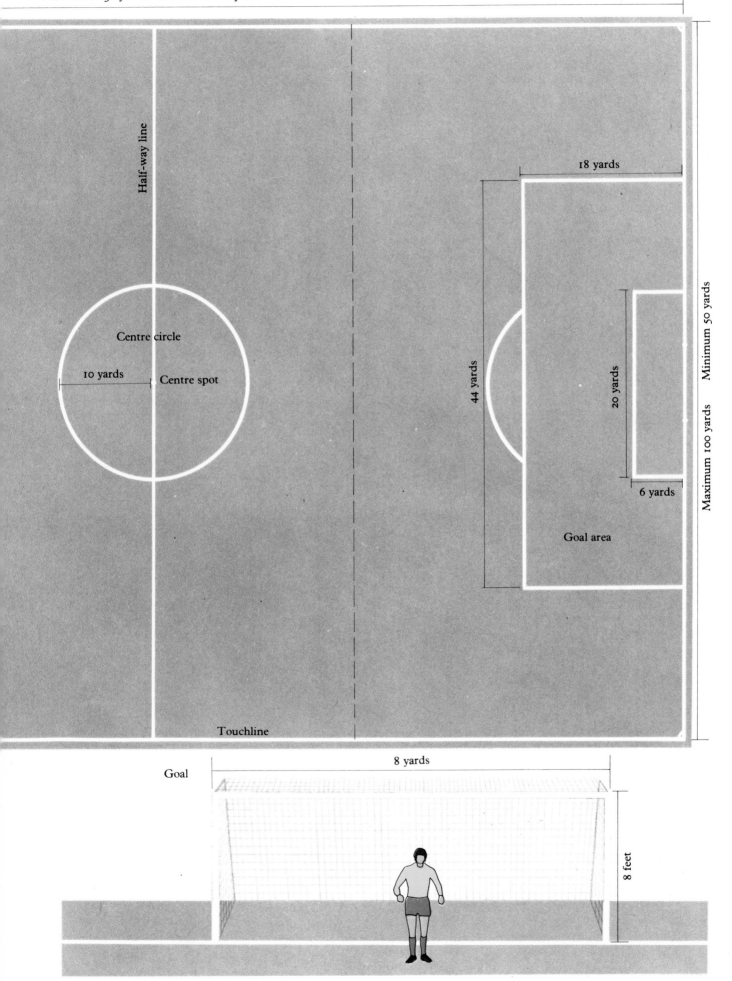

Maximum 130 yards   Minimum 100 yards

Half-way line

Centre circle

10 yards   Centre spot

Touchline

18 yards

44 yards

20 yards

6 yards

Goal area

Minimum 50 yards

Maximum 100 yards

Goal

8 yards

8 feet

79

remind defending players they must retreat ten yards from the ball, and he will signal this by raising both arms, palms upwards and fingers spread, to indicate the ten-yard rule. For an indirect free-kick or obstruction, he will stand with one arm down by his side and the other upraised, while to signal an award for hands he may tap one palm with a finger of the other hand.

He will illustrate that he is applying the advantage rule by extending both arms in front of his body and waving play on, and indicate a foul throw by going through the motions of the throw himself. For offside, you will see the referee stand and cross both arms in front of his body, forefingers extended, and for kicking, pushing and tripping he will make the appropriate movements, raising one foot well off the ground (kicking), extending both arms and making pushing signs (pushing), and slightly lifting one foot forward (to indicate tripping).

All these signals help to clarify refereeing decisions and, of course, the good referee does his best to ensure that the game flows, so that he is not the central figure, but rather an extension of the game itself.

Rules

There are 17 laws of the game, and they cover everything from the field of play to misconduct and fouls. Here, in simple terms, are the laws . . . and what they mean.

Law 1. This concerns the field of play, and covers the dimensions and the various areas, as illustrated by the diagram.

Law 2 concerns that vital piece of equipment without which there would be no game of Soccer – the ball. It must be spherical, of an approved material and colour, weigh between 14 and 16 ounces at the start of the game, and have a circumference of between 27 and 28 inches.

Law 3 refers to the number of players. Each team consists of not more than 11 players, one of whom must be the goalkeeper. In a League game, one substitute per side may be allowed for any reason at any time; in other competitions (such as European ties) the number of substitutes allowed may be higher.

Law 4 – Players' equipment, which consists of shirt, shorts, stockings and boots. The studs or bars in the boots must conform to safety regulations. The goalkeeper must wear colours which distinguish him from outfield players and from the referee, and approved colours for a goalkeeper's jersey are scarlet, royal blue, royal green or white.

Law 5 refers to referees. A referee is appointed for each game, and he is responsible for controlling that game. His decisions are final – once he has made a decision, it cannot be reversed.

Law 6 refers to the linesmen. Each linesman operates on opposite sides of the field and in separate halves, assisting the referee by indicating with the flag (each linesman's flag is of a different colour) when the ball is out of play and which side is entitled to a corner kick, goal kick or throw-in, or when there has been an infringement of the laws.

Law 7 concerns the duration of the game, which consists of two periods of 45 minutes, or two equal periods involving a lesser time, depending on the competition. The referee adds on time lost through stoppages for various reasons, and he can extend time for a penalty to be taken at or after normal time has expired in each half. There is also an interval between each period of play.

Law 8. Each team must be in its own half of the field, with the defending players at least 10 yards from the ball until it has been kicked. The flip of a coin (provided by the referee) by the captain of the home team, with the opposing captain calling, decides which team kicks off or which team chooses ends. The game cannot start until the ball has rolled its full circumference in a forward direction over the half-way line. When a goal is scored, it is the signal for the game to be restarted by the non-scoring side in the centre circle, as at the original kick-off, and immediately after the interval, the teams change ends and the game commences as it did initially, except that the kick-off is taken by the team other than that which began the match. A goal cannot be scored directly from a kick-off.

Law 9 dictates when the ball is in and out of play. It is out of play once it has wholly crossed the touchline or goal line, whether on the ground or in the air, and it is also 'dead' when the referee has halted the game for any other reason.

Law 10 is about the method of scoring. The referee signals a goal when the whole of the ball has passed over the goal line, between the goal posts and under the crossbar . . . provided, of course, that the referee is satisfied no infringement has occurred, such as an attacking outfield player having intentionally propelled the ball with his hand or arm.

Law 11 is the offside law. A player cannot be offside if he is in his own half of the field or receives the ball direct from a goal kick, a corner, a throw-in or a dropped ball. A player is declared offside, and penalized for being in an offside position, at the moment the ball touches or is played by one of his own team if, in the referee's view, he is interfering with play or with an opponent, or seeking to gain advantage by being in that position. He is in an offside position only if he is nearer his opponents' goal line than the ball.

Law 12 refers to misconduct and fouls, and there are nine instances where a player can be penalized. (1) If he intentionally kicks, or tries to kick, an opponent. (2) If he intentionally trips, or tries to trip, an opponent. (3) If he intentionally jumps at an opponent. (4) If he intentionally charges an opponent dangerously or violently. (5) If he intentionally charges an opponent from behind,

Linesmen assist the referee. If they notice an infringement they indicate by raising their flags. If the flag is not raised then, as far as the linesman, is concerned, no infringement has occurred.

unless the opponent is obstructing. (6) If he intentionally strikes, or tries to strike, an opponent. (7) If he intentionally pushes an opponent. (8) If he intentionally holds an opponent. (9) If he intentionally carries, strikes, or propels the ball with hand or arm (but this doesn't apply to the goalkeeper, so long as he is inside his own penalty area). A player guilty of any of these offences will have a direct free-kick awarded against him, and any one of these offences committed by a member of the defending team inside his own penalty area will result in a penalty award for the opposition.

If a player commits a lesser offence the referee can then award an indirect free-kick.

Law 13 – The free-kick. A direct free-kick is one from which a goal can be scored directly against the offending side; an indirect free-kick is one from which a goal cannot be scored, unless the ball is played or touched by a player other than the kicker before the ball passes through the goal. When a player takes a free-kick, all opposing players must stand at least ten yards away, but the kicker may not play the ball a second time until it has been touched or played by another player.

Law 14 – The penalty kick, which is a direct free-kick taken from the penalty spot. All players barring the penalty taker and the opposing goalkeeper must stay outside the penalty area and at least ten yards from the ball (note the arc at the edge of the penalty area) until the kick has been taken. The opposing 'keeper must stand on his own goal line between the posts, without moving.

Law 15 – the throw-in, which is taken when the ball has gone out of play, in the air or on the ground, by it wholly crossing the touchline. A player on the team opposite to that which put the ball out takes the throw from the spot where it went out of play, but no goal can be scored directly from a throw-in. The thrower must use both hands and deliver the ball from behind and over his head, and he must be facing the field of play, with part of each foot resting on the touchline or the ground outside the touchline at the moment of throwing the ball.

Law 16 – the goal kick, which is taken when the ball, in the air or on the ground, has wholly crossed the goal line outside the posts after having been last touched by a player from the attacking side. The ball is put back into play by a member of the defending team kicking it from the goal area on the side where the ball went out of play, and it must be kicked directly into play beyond the penalty area.

Law 17 – the corner kick, which is awarded when the ball, in the air or on the ground, has wholly crossed the goal line between goalpost and corner flag after having been last touched by a player of the defending side. The attacking team puts the ball back into play by one of its members taking the kick from within the quarter-circle of the corner on the side where the ball went out. A goal may be scored directly from a corner kick.

These are the 17 laws relating to the game of Soccer, but there is also what people inside the game call the 'unwritten 18th law'. Quite simply, two words describe it . . . 'common sense'.

Here we show the ways in which the referee indicates various offences. These signals are used by referees all over the world so that no matter what language a player talks, if he is penalized he will realize the reason for it by looking at the referee's signal. Below we show the equipment that every referee needs to take on to the pitch with him – two pencils, whistle, wristwatch, stopwatch, note pad, red card and yellow card.

Foul throw in

Hand-ball

Offside

Retire ten yards

Indirect free kick for obstruction

Player being sent off

Advantage

Tripping

Kicking

Pushing

THE GAME
WORLDWIDE

Football is not just a team game; it is a game played the world over. And once again, the 1978 World Cup produced some new stars for everyone to admire. Some of the games might have seemed a bit boring, and perhaps there was not much to see in the way of tactics, but England team-manager Ron Greenwood was right when he suggested that people inside the game could learn something from the matches. There is always something to learn, even if it seems that there may be nothing new.

As a matter of fact, while over the past few years we have become used to talking about 4-3-3 formations and so on, it was in a World Cup-tie away back in 1950 that a team turned to a 4-2-4 formation as they battled to beat Brazil in the final of the World Cup. That team was Uruguay, and they won the trophy for a second time, in the Maracana stadium in Rio de Janeiro.

Uruguay had gone behind very early in the second half, and it seemed Brazil were on the way to winning the World Cup. But the captain of Uruguay, Varela, who played at centre-half decided that drastic action, was needed, and so he began to move upfield. Twenty minutes after Brazil had scored, Varela began the move that brought Uruguay an equalizer.

He sent Ghiggia clear with a pass, and Brazil, who had been caught out pushing players into the opposition's half, were left stranded at the back as Ghiggia went on and hit a pass to Schiaffino, who was totally unmarked. Schiaffino did not miss such a chance to score, and it became Brazil 1, Uruguay 1. Varela continued to mastermind his team's attacking moves, and with only 11 minutes to go, Ghiggia got the ball, pushed a pass inside to Perez, and the right-winger whipped it into Brazil's net at lightning speed. That was the end of Brazil.

That was a long time ago, of course, and teams and patterns of play have altered in various ways. By 1966, British Soccer fans were hailing the achievements of their World Cup-winning team, especially striker Geoff Hurst, who scored a hat-trick in the Wembley final against West Germany, and Alan Ball, who did a magnificent job on the right in England's 4-3-3 formation. By 1970, everyone was talking again about Pele, and about his Brazilian team-mates such as Carlos Alberto, Tostao and Gerson; about Facchetti, Rivera and Riva, of Italy; about Seeler, Haller, Beckenbauer and Gerd Mueller, of West Germany.

In 1974, Scotland had high hopes of winning the World Cup, but in the end, although they never lost a match, they failed to reach the final, which was fought out by the host country, West Germany, and Holland, who had players such as Johan Cruyff and Johan Neeskens starring for them. West Germany won that tournament, but by 1978

Soccer is now catching on in a big way in the United States. This shot shows Carlos Alberto of New York Cosmos watching helplessly as a Tampa Bay Rowdy player has gone round his slide tackle.

Beckenbauer – 'Emperor Franz', as his fans called him – was no longer with Bayern Munich. He was playing for another star team in another continent – New York Cosmos, in the United States. And Cruyff, although still in Europe, but with Barcelona instead of Ajax, decided against going to Argentina.

Although the 1978 World Cup isn't long behind us, teams will be preparing over the next three years for the World Cup of 1982, and again we shall be looking for new stars. But right now, you might like to think of a World Cup team you would pick, based on the players you have seen and read about during the past few years. Almost certainly you would pick Cruyff and Beckenbauer; probably George Best, Bobby Charlton and Denis Law, as well.

Beckenbauer has proved one of the truly great players of the past few years, because he has shown that he can switch positions without losing any of his ability to stamp his authority on a game. He has always been an elegant-looking player, and he showed when he operated in midfield that he had a great deal of ability, when it came to making skilled passes aimed at setting his own attack going, or breaking through himself from a deep position to fire in a rocket-like shot for goal.

First capped in 1965, he became better known in the 1966 World Cup series, and as the years went by, he became world-famous for the way he could 'read' situations in a game, and get out of trouble

Denis Law, seen here playing for Manchester United, was one of the most adventurous attacking players of his generation. He was a member of Scotland's World Cup squad and played in Italy before joining 'United.

even inside his own penalty area. Beckenbauer, playing in the back-four line, would play his way out of danger just as well as he sized up likely moves from the opposition and cut them out before they had even threatened danger. He was one of the players signed by New York Cosmos when Pele was ready to retire, and another player signed by the American club, of course, was winger Dennis Tueart, the England international who was with Sunderland and Manchester City. Tueart has his own brand of skills – speed, the ability to beat a defender on the wing or cutting inside, bravery – and a cracking shot which has brought him loads of goals.

Talking of cracking shots, no-one could hit a ball harder than Bobby Charlton, and no-one could 'bend' a free-kick better than the Brazilian international, Roberto Rivelino, who played in the 1978 World Cup. Tueart, Charlton and Rivelino have also had another thing in common – the ability to hammer a fierce, accurate drive with the left foot. Just like Ferenc Puskas, the former Hungarian star, used to do.

On the other hand, Denis Law was noted for his ability to score goals 'out of nothing' with his head, and he was always a danger lurking inside the 18-yard box, ready to pop the ball into the net. He was

George Best, was one of the top attractions of the Aztecs, and is still one of the most exciting players in the world. His dazzling skills enable him to create chances out of nothing and he is still pulling the crowds in whenever he plays.

brave, too – he didn't 'duck' when defenders came flying in ready to make physical contact.

George Best was one of the famous forwards with Manchester United, and the former United goalkeeper, Harry Gregg – who himself was voted the world's No. 1 'keeper in the 1958 World Cup, when he played for Northern Ireland in Sweden – tells of a story of how he played against Best when George was a newcomer to United. It was in a practice session, and as Best shaped to shoot for goal, Harry Gregg 'showed' him a gap to aim for at one side. But Best didn't fall for the trick – he put the ball past the 'keeper at the opposite side. Beginner's luck, thought Harry Gregg; so soon after, in a similar situation, he did the same thing again, 'showing' Best a gap at which to aim. But again Best put the ball to the opposite side and that was when Gregg realized he had seen a youngster who was going to be something special in football.

Rodney Marsh was considered something special, too, by the Queen's Park Rangers and Manchester City supporters, and this former England international is another player who moved into US Soccer. He is still wowing them with Tampa Bay Rowdies, and his personal fan club calls itself 'The Marshist Society'.

Marsh, perhaps, was even more of an indivi-

dualist than Best. The Irishman, at the peak of his fame with Manchester United, would be all players rolled into one: he could win the ball off an opponent when helping out his own defence, take it forward, beat one, two or even three opposing defenders, then hammer in an unstoppable shot which would win the game. Marsh was not concerned so much with being an all-rounder, but he had his own, superb brand of trickery which bamboozled opposing players, and sometimes his own team-mates. Marsh has always enjoyed tricking players and giving the crowd something to enthuse about.

Earlier, I mentioned players such as Gerd Mueller and Johan Cruyff and Johan Neeskens. Mueller was not a player who considered his mission in life was simply to entertain. His job, as he saw it, was to stick the ball into the net – and how well he did that job for West Germany. At just over 5ft 9in, he was not the tallest of strikers; but he was always on the right spot at the right time, and it was seldom that he missed a scoring chance. Certainly, no defender could afford to give him a second chance.

Neeskens, too, who moved with Cruyff from Ajax to Barcelona, could stick the ball in the net as a striker, and he showed when he switched to midfield that he could make strong runs through to the opposition's 18-yard box and still get his name on the scoresheet. As for Cruyff, not for nothing did he gain a reputation as the world's No. 1 footballer in succession to Pele, and he has shown that he can score goals with head or feet. His positional sense is extraordinary, for he drifts around the field and makes space for himself, as well as getting into positions where he can take a pass from or put a pass to a team-mate. When Barcelona wanted to sign him, they had to pay Ajax £922,000 for the privilege!

The 1978 World Cup showed that Robbie Rensenbrink, who (although he is Dutch), plays for Anderlecht in Belgium, hadn't lost that ice-cool concentration which brings him so many goals, and we also saw another aspect of Holland's ability to play all-round football – Rudi Krol, who now operates as a 'sweeper' in the international side, can start attacks and crack in scoring efforts, as well. Considering that Krol played at full-back in Holland's 1974 World Cup side, it all goes to show what an adaptable footballer he is.

You may also remember a Peruvian player named Teofilo Cubillas – like Mueller, no giant – who scored some sensational goals, and the young Italian, Paolo Rossi, who impressed everyone with his swiftness to get into scoring positions and strike with deadly accuracy. And what about one of the Argentinian stars whom Tottenham Hotspur signed? Osvaldo Ardiles who, with his fellow-international, Ricardo Villa, quickly made an impact in his new country.

Ardiles and Villa were reputed to have cost a total of £700,000 when they joined Spurs, but they certainly drew the fans wherever they played. Ardiles was a key player in midfield for Argentina in the 1978 World Cup, and with more than 40 full caps he had rightly earned a high reputation. In fact, England team-manager Ron Greenwood described Ardiles as 'the best right-sided midfield player in the World Cup'.

Which brings us back to our starting point . . . and I hope I have shown you in the world-wide list of famous names that, once again, whether it's at the highest level or at your own level of play, doing 'what comes naturally' remains a part of the game of football, and if you have a natural talent it is there to be used. Throw in some hard work, and practise so that you become almost perfect at doing what suits you best, while not neglecting to work on those parts of your game which tend to be weak spots.

Soccer in the United States

Soccer in the United States takes a somewhat different approach than other countries do, partly because the game is still getting off the ground in the States, and they are trying hard to cater for the fans. For instance, each side of the field has a line across it 35 yards out from goal – and until you've crossed that line, you cannot be offside. There also has to be a definite result in a match, so if the game ends as a draw after 90 minutes, there is a short spell of extra time, and if things haven't reached a

conclusion, there is a shoot-out, on the lines of a penalty competition . . . but with this difference. Each team has five chances, with the attacking players starting with the ball on the 35-yard line and taking their shot within five seconds. The goalkeepers have no restrictions on movement during the five-second period.

If, after the five attempts, there is still no result, the teams continue to take alternate kicks until one side has scored more goals than the other after an equal number of attempts – although no player may take more than one kick until all the other eligible members of his side have made their attempts. So, eventually, a result is certain.

The North American Soccer League is certainly doing its utmost to woo supporters, and so are the clubs, who have names which might sound strange to English fans. For instance, The New England Teamen, Dallas Tornado, Philadelphia Fury, Los Angeles Aztecs, Detroit Express, Tulsa Roughnecks, Chicago Sting, Memphis Rogues and Tampa Bay Rowdies. The Rowdies, managed by former Millwall team-boss Gordon Jago, have a slogan which says 'Soccer is a kick in the grass', and you can see this slogan printed on the backs of tea-shirts worn by Rowdies fans.

Former top referee Gordon Hill – he was a head master at a Leicester school – is in charge of the youth programme at Tampa Bay, and when I was in America I talked to him about the way they are encouraging youngsters to take up the game. Gordon told me how the Rowdies run a summer camp for youngsters, about their plans to take youngsters to England on courses so that they can learn more about the game. 'I'm dealing with 14-year-olds who will be the future of the game here,' he said. 'There are thousands of kids spending summer kicking a ball around – Pele is running Soccer camps, too – and this means the game is really taking root.'

English managers are helping to popularize the game in the States – men like Freddie Goodwin, who is also president of the Minnesota Kicks club, Noel Cantwell (New England Teamen), Tony Waiters (Vancouver Whitecaps), Eddie Firmani (New York Cosmos) and Ken Furphy (Detroit Express). I also talked to players such as Dennis Tueart, Gordon Banks and Ian Callaghan, who were playing at the time for Fort Lauderdale Strikers, down on the south-east coast of Florida.

Dennis said: 'People are very much aware of Soccer, and my club, the Cosmos, must take a lot of the credit for upgrading the standard each year. It will take a few more years to get into the top bracket, and it's important that we don't get carried away and try to go too far too quickly. But it will come.'

Tony Currie of Leeds United successfully gets past Ian Bowyer of Nottingham Forest during an English League game.

Freddie Goodwin's verdict: 'The quality of play and coaches is improving every season. The number of youngsters playing Soccer has increased dramatically in the past three or four years, and I cannot see the game failing to grow in popularity every year. Top players from England, such as Trevor Francis, Charlie George and Alan Ball, have played for American clubs on loan, and I think American Soccer will entice more and more players over every year.'

Gordon Banks, who spent a couple of seasons with Fort Lauderdale Strikers (the club George Best joined from Los Angeles Aztecs), told me: 'The game is really taking off, and more and more youngsters are becoming involved'. And Ian Callaghan, who has won just about every honour in the game in England said, 'The standard is higher than I'd expected, although teams vary – there are a lot of English, German and Yugoslav players. The game is going to get better. In Fort Lauderdale, they're really Soccer-conscious, and they're playing it in the schools.'

American clubs stage their games with the kind of ballyhoo you don't see in Britain, but it is attracting parents, as well as youngsters. The family parks the car and has a picnic before the match, and when the players go out they often make a spectacular entrance. Fort Lauderdale Strikers, for instance, have taken the field on bikes, on a fire engine, on a Wells Fargo security 'stagecoach'. And there are the cheer leaders to get the fans enthusiastic about their team – the girls at Fort Lauderdale are called the 'Strikers' Psychers'.

Parents are being wooed, as they are told it's safer for their youngsters to play Soccer than some other long-established American sports. Cheaper, too, to kit out the kids. And Jim Trecker says: 'Thare are more than a million youngsters playing organized Soccer here, and we've been grooming our own national side. Soccer has taken root; many kids are turning away from American football. Our clubs will be touring Europe, and more and more we want a year-round involvement. We're growing all the time. And our hopes of qualifying for the 1982 World Cup finals are valid, because we're in one of the weaker groups.'

The Americans have certainly not been slow to use European know-how in their bid to establish Soccer, and dozens of players and managers have been spreading the gospel across the Atlantic, holding coaching 'clinics' for youngsters, as well as concentrating on getting results for their clubs. And girls, as well as boys, are being encouraged to play Soccer. One day, maybe soon, it will be a case of 'The Yanks are coming' . . . and they have not forgotten that in the 1950 World Cup, at a place called Belo Horizonte, the US team beat England 1–0 – and could well do so again.

Kenny Dalglish of Liverpool and Scotland, manages to fend off a tackle from Owen of Manchester City.

SOCCER MILESTONES

1863	The Football Association founded.
1871	Start of the FA Cup competition.
1872	Start of official international matches.
1873	Formation of Scottish Football Association.
1874	Introduction of shinguards.
1875	Introduction of crossbar.
1876	Formation of Football Association of Wales.
1878	Introduction of whistle used by referees.
1880	Formation of Irish Football Association.
1882	Formation of International Board.
1883	Introduction of two-handed throw-in.
1885	Professionalism in Soccer became legal.
1888	Formation of Football League.
1890	Formation of Irish League.
1891	Formation of Scottish League.
1891	Introduction of penalty kick.
1892	Formation of English Second Division.
1898	Introduction of promotion and relegation.
1901	Introduction of maximum wage.
1902	Formation of Welsh League.
1904	Formation of FIFA.
1905	First £1,000 transfer.
1908	Introduction of FA Charity Shield.
1911	Formation of Central League.
1913	United States Football Association affiliates to FIFA.
1914	Brooklyn Field Club win the first United States Soccer Federation National Open Challenge Cup.
1919	League extension to 44 clubs.
1920	Formation of Third Division (South).
1921	Formation of Third Division (North).
1922	Formation of Scottish League Second Division.
1923	First Cup final at Wembley.
1925	New offside law introduced.
1928	Britain left FIFA.
1928	First £10,000 transfer.
1930	First World Cup (winners were the host nation, Uruguay).
1933	American Soccer League formed.
1933	Kearny Irish won the first American Soccer League Championship.
1934	Italy won World Cup, as host nation.
1938	Italy retained World Cup, in France.
1939	Introduction of numbering of players.
1939	War brought suspension of all recognized Soccer competitions, although football continued on various levels.
1945	FA Cup competition resumed, as Soccer got under way again.
1946	Britain rejoined FIFA.
1950	Uruguay won World Cup, in Brazil.

1950	World record crowd of 200,000 in Rio de Janeiro at World Cup.
1950	Extension of Third Division to 48 clubs.
1950	U.S. Team beat England 1-0 in World Cup.
1954	West Germany won World Cup, in Switzerland.
1958	Manchester United aircrash at Munich.
1958	Brazil won World Cup, in Sweden.
1958	Introduction of four separate divisions in English League.
1961	Sir Stanley Rous became president of FIFA.
1962	Brazil won World Cup, in Chile.
1962	Manchester United set new record by paying £116,000 for Denis Law.
1964	318 people killed during a riot at the Argentina-Peru game at Lima.
1966	League allowed substitutes for injured players.
1966	England won World Cup at Wembley.
1967	Glasgow Celtic became first British club to win European Cup.
1968	North American Soccer League formed.
1968	Manchester United became first English club to win European Cup.
1970	Brazil won World Cup for third time, this time in Mexico.
1971	66 spectators killed during a Celtic-Rangers game at Ibrox when a barrier collapsed.
1974	West Germany, the host nation, won World Cup.
1977	United States won the Soccer Festival of America.
1977	Liverpool reached FA Cup final, won League championship and European Cup.
1977	Over 77,000 fans watch Cosmos play Fort Lauderdale Strikers in New Jersey.
1977	Liverpool sold Kevin Keegan to SV Hamburg for reputed £500,000, paid record fee of £440,000 to Glasgow Celtic for Kenny Dalglish.
1978	Liverpool reached League Cup final, finished runners-up to champions Nottingham Forest, and became first British club to retain European Cup.
1978	Argentina, the host nation, won the World Cup.
1978	Nottingham Forest break record for longest run in Football League without defeat: a total of 42 games. Their run was ended by a 2-0 defeat at Liverpool.
1978	More than 1,000,000 American children play in organized soccer leagues.

GLOSSARY

Here, in simple terms, is an explanation of words constantly used to describe various aspects of the game:

Advantage Application by the referee of the rule allowing a player to continue with the ball, even though he may have been impeded by an opponent. The referee applies the advantage rule instead of awarding a foul and thus halting play.

Back-pass When a player kicks the ball back to his goalkeeper or a defending team-mate.

Banana kick (or 'bending' the ball) When a player kicks the ball in such a way that it curves through the air.

Centre or cross Passing the ball from the right or left flank of the field into the centre of the pitch.

Charge Make shoulder-to-shoulder contact with an opponent.

Clear or clearance Kick or head the ball upfield and away from your own defensive area. A goalkeeper may throw the ball out.

Corner kick Free-kick taken from the corner flag at the extreme flank to the right or left of either goal.

Defender Player whose primary job is to prevent opponents getting past and scoring goals.

Defensive wall Line-up of players seeking to guard route to goal when opponent is taking a free-kick.

Dribble Taking the ball past an opponent by using body swerve and controlling the ball with one or both feet, or simply running with the ball and controlling it with the feet.

Eighteen-yard box Area marked out in front of and on each side of goal. If an attacker is unfairly brought down in this area, the referee can award a penalty or a free-kick.

Forward An attacking player whose main task is to create scoring chances or score goals himself.

Foul An unfair method of stopping an opponent.

Free-kick Exactly what it says . . . a free-kick to the team when the opposition has halted play by unfair means. At a free-kick, opponents must retreat ten yards and stay there until the ball has been kicked. A direct free-kick means the player can shoot directly for goal; an indirect free-kick means the ball be must played by a second man before a shot can be taken.

Goalkeeper The only man who can use his hands to take the ball, although he must do this only inside the 18-yard box. If he goes outside the box, he must kick or head the ball. He is the team's last line of defence.

Hands Intentional (and illegal) handling of the ball with hand or arm.

Header Using the head to make contact with the ball.

Kick-off The initial act of starting the game (the ball must roll forward for its full circumference before it can be in play).

Laying it off Taking a pass and immediately playing the ball to a team-mate.

Link-man Alternative name for a midfield player.

Lob A kick which lofts the ball into the air. Where the ball is kicked precisely, over a defender to a team-mate, or over a goalkeeper into goal, it is a chip.

Marking Keeping close watch on an opponent.

Midfield man A player who operates between his own defence and attack, either as a ball-winner who stops opponents or as a creator of attacks by making shrewd passes to his own team-mates. He is the link between defence and attack, and operates offensively or defensively, as the occasion demands.

Nutmegging Pushing the ball between an opponent's legs, then running round him to regain possession.

Obstruction Using the body to prevent an opponent from going round you.

Offside Being in a position in the opponents' half of the field where you cannot legally play the ball.

Overlap When a defender goes down the flank (with or without the ball) and by-passes a team-mate during an attacking foray.

Pass Hitting the ball accurately to a team-mate, or pushing the ball into space so that a team-mate can run on to it. A square pass is one where the ball is pushed directly to right or left for a team-mate; a diagonal pass is made forward at an angle; a reverse pass is one which is sent in the opposite direction to which the man making the pass is running.

Penalty A free-kick where the ball is placed on the marked penalty spot directly facing the goalkeeper, who must not move until the kick has been taken. No opponents may stand between the penalty taker and the goalkeeper.

Penalty area Otherwise known as the 18-yard box.

Park or pitch Common names for the field of play.

Save When a scoring attempt is foiled by the goalkeeper catching, stopping or deflecting the ball, or a defender stops or deflects the ball from goal with head or feet.

Selling a dummy Kidding an opponent you are going to do one thing, then doing something else.

Set-piece When the game is brought to a halt and the team with the advantage is awarded a free-kick, a corner or a throw-in.

Shielding Keeping possession of the ball and using your body to screen the ball from your opponent.

Six-yard box An area marked out in front and on each side of goal.

Striker An attacking player, usually operating in a position directly in front of goal, whose job it is to get the ball into the net.

Support Helping a team-mate who has the ball by making yourself available to receive a pass.

Sweeper A defender who plays ahead of or behind the defensive line to pick up the ball when it goes loose.

Tackle Trying to gain possession of the ball from your opponent with the foot, when the ball is at his feet.

Target man An attacking player, usually good at winning the ball in the air, who makes himself available in and around the opposition's 18-yard box to take passes from team-mates.

Throw-in An advantage awarded by the referee to a team where the ball has gone out of play off an opponent, and the taker of the throw can use his hands to direct the ball to a team-mate.

INDEX

ACKNOWLEDGEMENTS

Photography by Harry Ormesher

Additional photographs by kind permission of:
All-Sport: 60–1, (Don Morley) 88;
Colorsport: Endpapers, 1, 8–9, 10–11, 25, 28–9, 76–7, 86–7, 90–1; FMS-Fotos: 84–5;
Pressefoto Rzepka: 44–5; Sven Simon: 2–3.

Illustrations by Paul Buckle

PDO 79-141